29.133 Xml

...aircraft 1...3,
8/-
629.

The Pocket Encyclopaedia of World Aircraft in Colour

# PIONEER AIRCRAFT
## 1903–1914

The Pocket Encyclopaedia
of World Aircraft in Colour

# PIONEER AIRCRAFT

## 1903–1914

by

KENNETH MUNSON

Illustrated by
JOHN W. WOOD
Norman Dinnage
Brian Hiley
William Hobson
Tony Mitchell
Jack Pelling

LONDON
BLANDFORD PRESS

First Published in 1969
Copyright © 1969 Blandford Press Ltd.
167 High Holborn, London, w.c.1

Colour printed by The Ysel Press, Deventer, Holland
Text printed and books bound in England
by Richard Clay (The Chaucer Press), Ltd.,
Bungay, Suffolk

# PREFACE

In many ways, *Pioneer Aircraft* has been the most fascinating and instructive volume we have yet undertaken in this series, and one in which the necessity to restrain our selection of aircraft to eighty colour pages was more than usually difficult. However, those presented do, I believe, represent the major designs of historical significance to appear during this formative period, together with one or two of the more bizarre outlines that were also prevalent at the time. Many of the pioneers' other designs, which space prevented us from illustrating, are referred to in the main text.

As might be imagined, one of the primary difficulties in preparing this particular volume was the production of reliable general arrangement drawings, for between 1903 and 1914 such documents were often either of a very sketchy nature or were entirely non-existent. It is due in no small measure to the co-operation of many of the individuals named below, as well as to the efforts of our team of artists, that this problem was overcome so successfully. Only in two cases have we felt that the information at our disposal was an insufficient basis for reliable plan and side elevations; in several other cases, such drawings are appearing, I believe, for the first time since the existence of the aircraft which they portray.

If ever there was a belief that aeroplanes built before World War 1 were uniformly lacking in character or colour, this volume should swiftly dispel such an illusion, and for his unrivalled knowledge of these early finishes we are again deeply indebted to Ian D. Huntley. Special thanks are also due to Messrs. C. H. Gibbs-Smith and J. M. Bruce, for their kindness in reading the manuscript and offering much helpful comment and advice; and to John W. R. Taylor for making possible an extensive study of contemporary technical journals. Among the many others whose help was invaluable in bringing the whole project to fruition were Pamela Matthews, and Ann Tilbury of *Flight International*; Messrs. Charles F. Andrews of British Aircraft Corporation; John W. Bingham of the Smithsonian Institution, Washington; R. W.

Bradford of the National Museum of Canada; Lennart Ege; H. F. Ellehammer of the Ellehammers Laboratorium, Denmark; Jørgen Lundø of Politikens Forlag, Copenhagen; Harald J. Penrose; Col. J. Rougevin-Baville of the Musée de l'Air, Paris; Oliver J. Tapper; Stanley M. Ulanoff; John W. Wickenden; and the staffs of the Public Record Office and the Science Museum in London. Acknowledgment is also made of certain items published in the U.S. journal *Air Progress*, and in the Journal of the American Aviation Historical Society; and to the Editor of *Flight International* for permission to reproduce the extract from *Flight* appearing on pp. 7–11.

May 1968

# INTRODUCTION

## Wing-Warping

The question of controlling an aeroplane laterally, whether for the purpose of causing it deliberately to turn to left or right or simply to maintain it on an even keel without rolling, was one of the cardinal problems besetting the early pioneers of heavier-than-air flight. In this connection it may be of interest to read a description of the system of wing-warping introduced on the 1902 Wright Glider and subsequently patented by Orville and Wilbur Wright (Pat. No. 6732, applied for on 23 March 1903). Wing-warping was not, in itself, an invention of the Wrights; what was significant was their improvement, arrived at by Orville Wright, of linking the warp-control cables with a single, hinged rudder, so that the latter surface was automatically pulled over when the wings were warped, thus offsetting the increased drag of the dropped wings and permitting the aeroplane to make a banked turn smoothly and naturally.

The essence of this system (which they modified later) is described in the following shortened version of the 1903 Patent, as published in *Flight* of 22 January 1910 and previously in the *The Automotor Journal*:

> The objects of our invention are, first, to provide a structure combining lightness, strength, convenience of construction, and the least possible edge of resistance; second, to provide means for maintaining or restoring the equilibrium of the apparatus; and, third, to provide efficient means of guiding the machine in both vertical and horizontal directions. We obtain these objects by the mechanism shown in the accompanying drawing, in which Fig. 1 is a view in perspective of the machine, Fig. 2 a side elevation, and Fig. 3 a top plan view.
>
> The superposed horizontal surfaces, A, formed by stretching cloth upon frames of wood and wire, constitute the 'wings' or supporting part of the apparatus. They are connected to each other through hinge-joints by upright standards and lateral

7

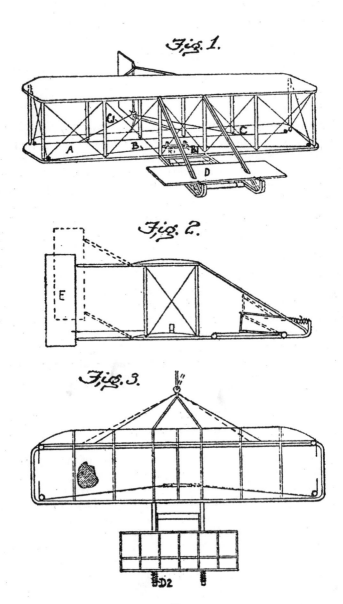

Fig. 1.

Fig. 2.

Fig. 3.

stay-wires, which, together with lateral spars of the wing framing, form truss systems, giving the whole machine a great transverse rigidity and strength. The hinge-joints admit of both flexing and twisting movements, and may be either ball and socket joints or any joint of sufficiently loose construction to admit of the movements specified. The object of joints having both flexing and twisting movement is to permit superposed wing surfaces, or parts thereof, when joined together by upright standards, to be twisted or bent out of their normal planes for the purpose hereafter specified. We do not restrict ourselves to the use of any particular form of joint, nor to its use at any particular number of places.

One end of the rope, B, is attached near the rear corner of the upper surface, passes diagonally downward around pulleys, and diagonally upward to the corresponding corner at the opposite end of the machine. The rope, C, is attached to the front corner of the upper surface, passes around pulleys, and back to the opposite upper corner. The movable cradle, $B_1$, is attached to the rope, B, at the point where the operator's body rests, and provides a means of imparting movement to the ropes, B and C. The operator lies prone on the lower surface, his hips resting in the cradle, and his hands grasping the roller, $D_1$, which actuates the front rudder, D. The ropes maintain the fore and aft positions of the two surfaces, A, with respect to each other, and by their movement impart a twist to the entire structure, including the wings, A; when the cradle is moved to right or left by the operator, the motion is communicated through the ropes and the upright standards in such a manner that the wing surfaces are twisted, the rear edge of the wing tips being drawn downward at one end of the machine and drawn upward at the other, thus presenting the left set of wing tips to the wind at a greater or less angle than the right. When in flight, the end having the greater angle will necessarily rise and the other end will sink, so that the lateral balance of the machine is under control through twisting movements of the wing tips by the operator, by means of the cradle.

The flexible front rudder, D, is mounted upon struts by attachment to the cross-stick, which is located near the centre of pressure, so as to form a balanced rudder. The up-and-down motion of the front edge of the rudder is in part restrained by springs, D2. The rear edge is raised and lowered by means of the axles, D1. The restraining action of the springs causes the ribs to bend when the rear edge is raised or lowered, thus presenting a concave surface to the action of the wind, and very greatly increasing its power as compared with a plane of equal area. By regulating the pressure on the upper and lower sides of the rudder, through changes of angle and curvature, a turning movement is communicated to the main structure and the course of the machine is directed upward or downward at the will of the operator, and the longitudinal balance maintained. Contrary to the usual custom, we place the horizontal rudder in front of the main surfaces or 'wings' at a negative angle, and use no horizontal tail at all. By this arrangement we obtain a forward surface which is almost free from pressure under ordinary conditions of flight, but which, even if not moved at all, becomes an efficient lifting surface whenever the speed of the machine is accidentally reduced very much below the normal, and thus largely counteracts that backward travel of the centre of pressure on the main surfaces or wings, which has frequently been productive of serious injuries by causing the machine to turn downward and strike the ground head on. We are aware that a forward horizontal rudder of different construction has been used in combination with a supporting surface and a rear horizontal rudder, but this combination was not intended to effect and did not effect the object which we obtained by the arrangement of surfaces here described.

The vertical tail or rudder, E, is attached through universal joints to two pairs of struts, which lie in parallel, horizontal planes and are connected to the rear edges of the main surfaces by hinged joints. This combination secures the tail rigidly in a vertical position, but enables it to turn on a vertical axis, and also to rise bodily in case it strikes the ground and thus escape breakage. The cords, B1, are tiller-ropes which connect the rudder-wheel to the rope, C, which, in conjunction with the rope, B, imparts the twisting motion to the wing tips as heretofore described. By this method of attachment the same motion of the ropes which activates the wing tips also presents to the wind that side of the vertical rear-rudder which is toward the tip having the smaller angle of incidence. The wing tip presented to the wind at the greater angle, under the usual conditions of flight, has both greater lift and greater drift, or resistance, than the other. The wing with the greater angle, therefore, tends to rise and drop behind, while the other sinks and moves ahead. Under these circumstances the longitudinal axis of the machine tends to turn toward the wing having the greater angle, while the general course of the machine through the air tends toward that wing which is the lowest, with the result that a wide divergence soon arises between the direction which the machine faces and its actual direction of travel. By the use of a rear movable vertical rudder, so operated as to present to the wind that side which is toward the wing having the least angle, we obtain a turning force opposite to and greater than that arising from the difference in the resistance of the two wings, and thus are able to keep the longitudinal axis of the machine approximately in coincidence with the line of flight.

The principal claims are: the use of jointed standards, diagonal stay-wires, and a device for twisting the surfaces.

# SOME MAJOR AEROPLANE COMPETITIVE
# EVENTS OF 1908–1914

### British Military Aircraft Trials

Held at Larkhill, Salisbury Plain, during August 1912. Thirty-one entrants originally, but owing to withdrawals for various reasons the effective competitors were reduced to nineteen. From these, the Cody biplane was declared winner of both the 'Open' and the 'All British' prizes, totalling £5,000.

### Circuit of Britain

Sponsored by the London *Daily Mail*. The race, open to all comers, was for a £10,000 first prize, and took place over a 1,010 mile (1,625·4 km.) course (Brooklands–Hendon–Harrogate–Newcastle –Edinburgh–Stirling–Glasgow–Carlisle–Manchester–Bristol–Exeter–Salisbury Plain–Brighton–Brooklands). Pilots were not allowed to change aircraft en route, and had to complete the journey in a maximum of 24 hours flying time. The race began on 22 July 1911 and was won by Lieutenant Jean Conneau of the French Navy ('André Beaumont') in a Blériot monoplane, who successfully regained Brooklands four days later with a total flying time of 22 hours 29 minutes 26 seconds.

The second Circuit of Britain, open between 16–30 August 1913, was a contest for all-British seaplanes flown by British pilots. To be flown over a nine-stage course (Southampton–Ramsgate–Yarmouth–Scarborough–Aberdeen–Cromarty–Oban–Dublin–Falmouth–Southampton) totalling 1,540 miles (2,478·4 km.), and completed within 72 hours of starting. There were four entrants, but only one starter: Harry Hawker in a Sopwith tractor seaplane. The £5,000 first prize was not awarded, but Hawker was given a special personal award of £1,000 for his achievement in completing 1,043 miles (1,678·5 km.) of the circuit in approximately 22 hours flying time before having to withdraw after sustaining an accident when he had almost completed the Oban–Dublin leg of the journey.

A third competition, scheduled for 1–15 August 1914, was cancelled owing to the outbreak of war.

## Circuit of Europe

Competition for cash prizes totalling £18,300. Held between 18 June and 7 July 1911 (though scheduled originally to last only twelve days). Main stages were Paris (start and finish)–Liège–Utrecht–Brussels–Roubaix–Calais–London–Calais–Paris, the total distance being approximately 1,000 miles (1,600 km.). Pilots were allowed to change aircraft en route. Race won by Lieutenant Jean Conneau of the French Navy ('André Beaumont') in a Blériot monoplane.

## Gordon Bennett Aviation Trophy

Speed competition, held five times before World War 1, each race taking place in the home country of the previous year's winner. First held at Rheims, France, on 28 August 1909 and won by Glenn Curtiss, who covered two laps of a 10 km. (6·2 mile) course in 15 minutes 50·4 seconds in the Golden Flyer fitted with a 50 h.p. engine. The 1910 race, over 20 laps of a 5 km. (3·1 mile) course, was held at Belmont Park, New York, on 29 October 1910. The course was completed by Claude Grahame-White, flying a Blériot monoplane, in a winning time of 1 hour 1 minute 4·74 seconds. In 1911 the race was held on 1 July over a 25-lap course at Eastchurch totalling 94 miles (151·3 km.), and was won by C. T. Weymann in a Nieuport monoplane with a time of 1 hour 11 minutes 36·2 seconds. Jules Védrines, in a Deperdussin monoplane, completed the 200 km. (124·3 mile) course at Chicago on 10 September 1912 in 1 hour 10 minutes 56·85 seconds. The final pre-war Gordon Bennett race, at Rheims on 29 September 1913, was also over 200 km. and was won in 59 minutes 45·6 seconds by Maurice Prévost in a Deperdussin monoplane.

## Michelin Trophies

The first of the annual aviation trophies awarded by the Michelin Tyre Company for duration flying was open to all comers, and was won by Wilbur Wright, who on 31 December 1908 completed 56 laps of a 2·2 km. (1·37 mile) circuit in France, establishing at the same time world records both for duration and for distance flown.

Subsequent competitions, open only to British pilots flying all-British aircraft, were for the British Empire Michelin Cups Nos. 1 and 2. Five awards of Cup No. 1 were made prior to 1914, the prize on each occasion being £500. The first was won by J. T. C. Moore-Brabazon on 1 March 1910, for a flight of 19 miles (30·6 km.) in 31 minutes at Eastchurch in a Short biplane. On 31 December 1910 the second award was won by S. F. Cody for a flight of 185·46 miles (298·47 km.) in 4 hours 47 minutes at Laffan's Plain in his own biplane. Cody also won the third of these awards, for his flight – again round a Laffan's Plain circuit – of 261·5 miles (420·8 km.) on 29 October 1911. The next year, the award was made to Harry Hawker for his flight on 24 October 1912 of 8 hours 23 minutes in a Sopwith-Howard Wright biplane – a new British endurance record. The last pre-war award was made to R. H. Carr, who flew 315 miles (507 km.) in a Grahame-White Type X Charabanc on 6 November 1913.

In 1911 a second contest was introduced, for the British Empire Michelin Cup No. 2, to run for three years with progressively increasing prizes of £400, £600 and £800. It was to be flown round a cross-country circuit, the total distance being increased annually, and the winner being the pilot with the fastest non-stop time. The first award went to S. F. Cody, who on 11 September 1911 was the only competitor to finish the 125 mile (201·2 km.) course, in 3 hours 7 minutes 30 seconds. Cody also won the 1912 award, on this occasion (12 October 1912) taking 3 hours 23 minutes to complete a 186 mile (299·3 km.) course. In 1913, when the course length was 279 miles (449 km.), no entrant completed the course and no award was made.

## Mortimer Singer Prizes

In 1911 Mortimer Singer offered prizes of £500 each to the Army and Navy pilots who could fly the greatest distance non-stop, carrying a passenger, before 31 March 1912. The Army prize was awarded to Lieutenant B. H. Barrington-Kennett, R.E., who covered 249·5 miles (401·5 km.) at Salisbury Plain in a Nieuport monoplane on 14 February 1912. Pilot of the winning Navy aircraft, a modified Short S.27 biplane, was Lieutenant A. H. Longmore, R.N., who covered 172 miles (276·8 km.) at Eastchurch on 1 December 1911.

In 1913, Mr. Singer put up another £500, this time to be won by an all-British amphibious aircraft after an exacting test. This involved six consecutive out-and-back flights between two points 5 miles (8·05 km.) apart, one of which was to be on land and the other on water. At each point the aircraft had to land before resuming its journey, and the entire twelve stages had to be completed within 5 hours of starting. Moreover, the aircraft had to attain a height of 1,500 ft. (457 m.) on one flight and at least 750 ft. (229 m.) on all of the others. The prize was won by Harry Hawker, flying the Sopwith Bat Boat between Hamble and the Solent, who completed the course in 3 hours 25 minutes.

## Schneider Trophy

Offered by M. Jacques Schneider for an international seaplane competition, the award consisting of a trophy valued at 25,000 frs. (approximately £1,000) and, for the first three years, a cash prize of 25,000 frs. to the winner. First contest, staged as an adjunct to the annual seaplane meeting at Monaco, was held on 15 April 1913 and consisted of 28 laps of a 10 km. (6·2 mile) course. Won by Maurice Prévost in a Deperdussin float monoplane in the official time of 3 hours 48 minutes 22 seconds (average speed 45·75 m.p.h. = 73·63 km/hr.). The following year's contest, over a course of the same length, was held on 20 April 1914, and was won by Howard Pixton in the Sopwith Schneider floatplane in 2 hours 0 minutes 13·4 seconds (average speed 86·78 m.p.h. = 139·66 km/hr.).

## United Kingdom Aerial Derby

Sponsored by the London *Daily Mail*, and flown over a circuit-of-London course starting and finishing at Hendon. Competition was for a 100 guinea trophy and cash prizes totalling £460 (first prize £250). First held on 8 June 1912, when the course length was 81 miles (130·4 km.) and the race was awarded (after an appeal) to T. O. M. Sopwith in a 2-seat Blériot monoplane, who returned a time of 1 hour 23 minutes 8·4 seconds. For the following year's race, held on 20 September 1913, the course was lengthened to 94·5 miles (152·1 km.); the winner was Gustav Hamel in a Morane-Saulnier monoplane, who finished in a time of 1 hour 15 minutes 49 seconds. Another Morane-Saulnier, flown by W. L. Brock, won the third Aerial Derby on 6 June 1914 with a time of 1 hour 18 minutes 54 seconds over the same course.

# THE COLOUR PLATES

As an aid to identification, the eighty colour plates which follow have been arranged on a visual basis, within the broad sequence: pusher monoplanes, pusher biplanes, tractor monoplanes, tractor biplanes, tractor triplanes and multiplanes. The 'split' plan view gives upper and lower surface markings within a single outline, but for the sake of clarity some of the less important wire bracing may be omitted, and asymmetric features such as offset pilots' seats may be shown in one aspect only. The reference number of each plate corresponds to the appropriate text matter, which is arranged alphabetically. An index to all types illustrated, and to others mentioned in the main text, appears on page 177.

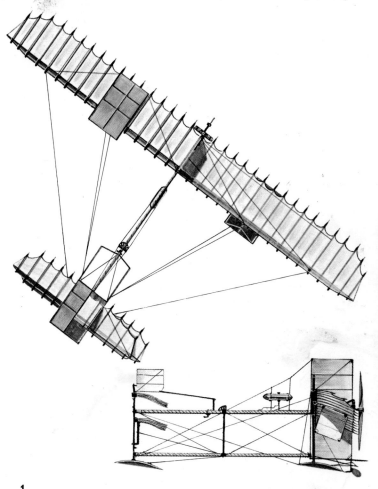

**1**

Henri Fabre *Hydravion,* March 1910. *Engine:* One 50 h.p. Gnome 7-cylinder rotary. *Span:* 45 ft. 11⅜ in. (14·00 m.). *Length:* 27 ft. 10⅝ in. (8·50 m.). *Height:* approx. 12 ft. 1¾ in. (3·70 m.). *Wing area:* 182·99 sq. ft. (17·00 sq. m.). *Take-off weight:* 1,047 lb. (475 kg.). *Speed:* 55 m.p.h. (89 km./hr.). *Airframe:* ash. *Propeller:* mahogany. *Covering:* plywood (floats) and cotton canvas.

# VALKYRIE (U.K.)

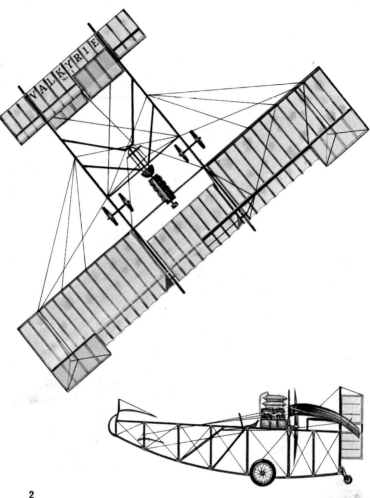

**2**

Aeronautical Syndicate (Barber) Valkyrie No. 1 (Type A), autumn 1910. *Engine:* One 35 h.p. Green 4-cylinder water-cooled in-line. *Span:* 34 ft. 0 in. (10·36 m.). *Length:* 22 ft. 0 in. (6·71 m.). *Height:* 8 ft. 6 in. (2·59 m.). *Wing area:* 190 sq. ft. (17·65 sq. m.). *Loaded weight (without pilot):* 520 lb. (236 kg.). *Speed:* approx. 45 m.p.h. (72 km./hr.). *Airframe:* Honduras mahogany and ash. *Propeller:* mahogany. *Covering:* unproofed Egyptian cotton.

## BOREL MONOPLANE (France)

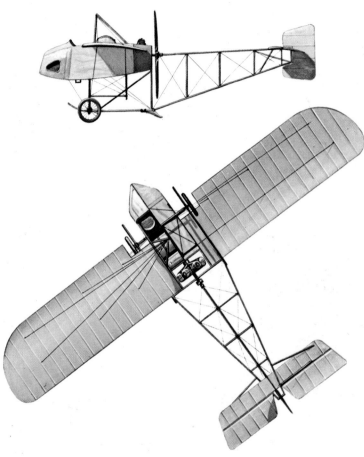

**3**

Borel military pusher monoplane, summer 1913. *Engine:* One 80 h.p. Gnome
7-cylinder rotary. *Span:* 36 ft. 9 in. (11·20 m.). *Length:* 24 ft. 5⅓ in. (7·45 m.).
*Height:* 9 ft. 2¼ in. (2·80 m.). *Wing area:* 204·5 sq. ft. (19·00 sq. m.). *Take-off
weight:* 926 lb. (420 kg.). *Airframe:* steel tube and ash. *Propeller:* mahogany.
*Covering:* aluminium (front and rear of nacelle), plywood (centre of nacelle)
and rubber-proofed fabric (wings and tail).

# SANTOS-DUMONT 14bis (Brazil/France)

**4**

Santos-Dumont 14*bis* as flown at Bagatelle, 12 November 1906. *Engine:* One 50 h.p. Antoinette 8-cylinder water-cooled Vee-type. *Span:* 36 ft. 9 in. (11·20 m.). *Length:* 31 ft. $9\frac{7}{8}$ in. (9·70 m.). *Height:* approx. 11 ft. $1\frac{7}{8}$ in. (3·40 m.). *Wing area:* 560 sq. ft. (52·00 sq. m.). *Take-off weight:* 661 lb. (300 kg.). *Speed:* approx. 25 m.p.h. (40 km./hr.). *Airframe:* pine and bamboo. *Propeller:* steel shafts, aluminium blades. *Covering:* unbleached cotton.

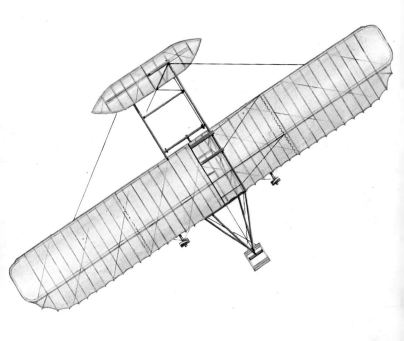

**5**

Wright Flyer I, as flown at Kill Devil Hills, North Carolina, 17 December 1903 (shown without launching rail). *Engine:* One 12 h.p. Wright 4-cylinder water-cooled in-line. *Span:* 40 ft. 4 in. (12·29 m.). *Length:* 21 ft. 1 in. (6·43 m.). *Height:* approx. 8 ft. 0 in. (2·44 m.). *Wing area:* 510 sq. ft. (47·38 sq. m.). *Empty weight:* 605 lb. (274 kg.). *Take-off weight:* approx. 750 lb. (340 kg.). *Speed:* approx. 30 m.p.h. (48 km./hr.). *Airframe:* spruce and ash. *Propellers:* spruce. *Covering:* 'Pride of the West' unbleached muslin.

## WRIGHT FLYER III (U.S.A.)

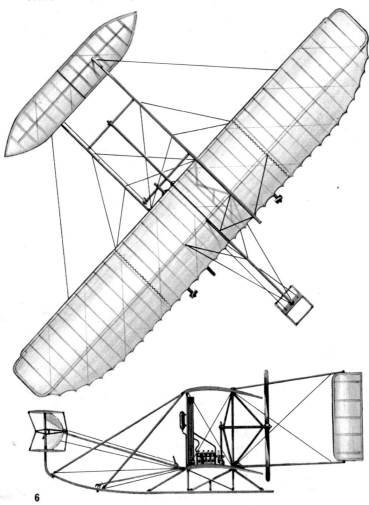

**6**

Wright Flyer III, *ca.* summer/autumn 1905. *Engine:* One 20 h.p. (approx.) Wright 4-cylinder water-cooled in-line. *Span:* 40 ft. 6 in. (12·34 m.). *Length:* 28 ft. 0 in. (8·53 m.). *Height:* approx. 8 ft. 0 in. (2·44 m.). *Wing area:* 503 sq. ft. (46·73 sq. m.). *Take-off weight:* approx. 855 lb. (388 kg.). *Speed:* approx. 35 m.p.h. (56 km./hr.). *Airframe:* spruce and ash. *Propellers:* spruce. *Covering:* bleached cotton.

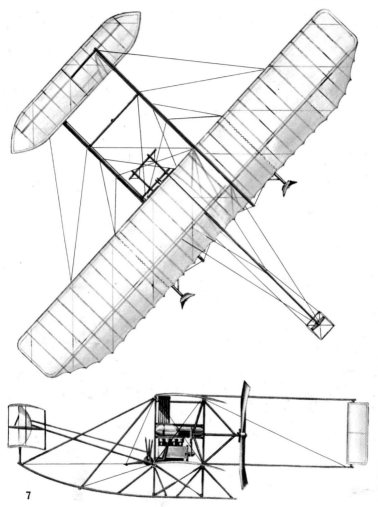

7

Wright Military Flyer (modified Type A) as tested at Fort Myer July 1909 and later designated Signal Corps No. 1. *Engine:* One 30 h.p. Wright 4-cylinder water-cooled in-line. *Span:* 36 ft. 6 in. (11·13 m.). *Length:* 28 ft. 11 in. (8·81 m.). *Height:* 8 ft. 1 in. (2·46 m.). *Wing area:* 415 sq. ft. (38·55 sq. m.). *Empty weight:* 740 lb. (336 kg.). *Take-off weight:* 1,200 lb. (544 kg.). *Speed:* 44 m.p.h. (71 km./hr.). *Airframe:* spruce and ash. *Propellers:* spruce. *Covering:* unbleached cotton.

# DE HAVILLAND BIPLANE (U.K.)

**8**

First de Havilland biplane, early 1910. *Engine:* One 45 h.p. Iris-built de Havilland 4-cylinder horizontally opposed piston engine. *Span:* 36 ft. 0 in. (10·97 m.). *Length:* 29 ft. 0 in. (8·84 m.). *Height:* approx. 9 ft. 10 in. (3·00 m.). *Wing area:* 408 sq. ft. (37·90 sq. m.). *Take-off weight:* 850 lb. (386 kg.). *Airframe:* American white pine, spruce and ash. *Propeller:* steel shafts, aluminium blades. *Covering:* undoped bleached cotton.

## BIRD OF PASSAGE (France)

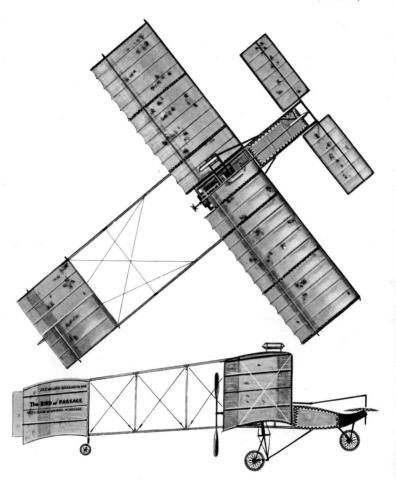

**9**

Voisin biplane *Bird of Passage*, ordered by Henry Farman but sold to J. T. C. Moore-Brabazon, 1909. *Engine:* One 60 h.p. E.N.V. Type F 8-cylinder water-cooled Vee-type. *Span:* 32 ft. 9¾ in. (10·00 m.). *Length:* 34 ft. 5⅝ in. (10·50 m.). *Height:* approx. 11 ft. 0 in. (3·35 m.). *Wing area:* 445 sq. ft. (41·34 sq. m.). *Take-off weight:* 1,150 lb. (522 kg.). *Speed:* 34 m.p.h. (55 km./hr.). *Airframe:* ash and steel tube. *Propeller:* steel shafts, aluminium blades. *Covering:* un-bleached cotton.

## VOISIN RACER (France)

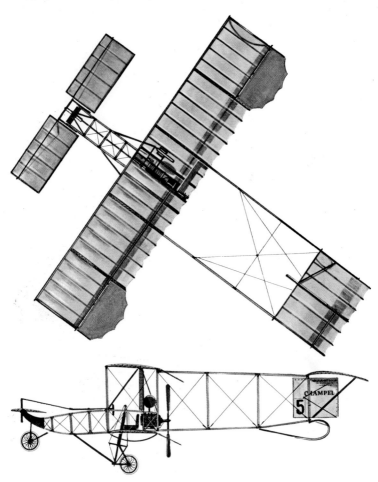

**10**

Voisin racing biplane flown by M. Champel at the Lanark meeting, August 1910. *Engine:* One 60 h.p. E.N.V. Type F 8-cylinder water-cooled Vee-type. *Span:* 29 ft. 6⅜ in. (9·00 m.). *Length:* 29 ft. 6⅜ in. (9·00 m.). *Height:* approx. 11 ft. 0 in. (3·35 m.). *Wing area:* 355·21 sq. ft. (33·00 sq. m.). *Take-off weight:* 921 lb. (418 kg.). *Speed:* approx. 45 m.p.h. (72 km./hr.). *Airframe:* ash and steel tube. *Propeller:* metal. *Covering:* Continental rubberised fabric.

## VOISIN BIPLANE (France)

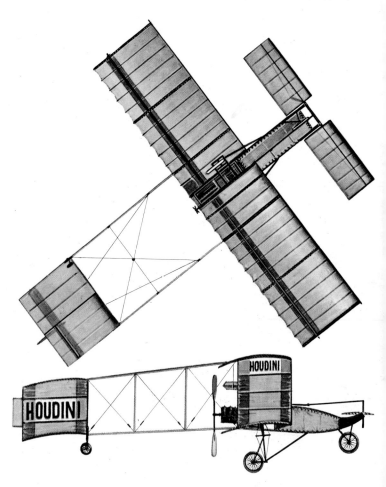

**11**

Standard type Voisin biplane, owned by Harry Houdini, *ca.* November/December 1909. *Engine:* One 60 h.p. E.N.V. Type F 8-cylinder water-cooled Vee-type. *Span:* 32 ft. 9¾ in. (10·00 m.). *Length:* 39 ft. 4½ in. (12·00 m.). *Height:* approx. 11 ft. 0 in. (3·35 m.). *Wing area:* 430·56 sq. ft. (40·00 sq. m.). *Take-off weight:* 1,323 lb. (600 kg.). *Speed:* 34 m.p.h. (55 km./hr.). *Airframe:* ash and steel tube. *Propeller:* steel shafts, aluminium blades. *Covering:* Continental rubberised fabric.

**FARMAN III (France)**

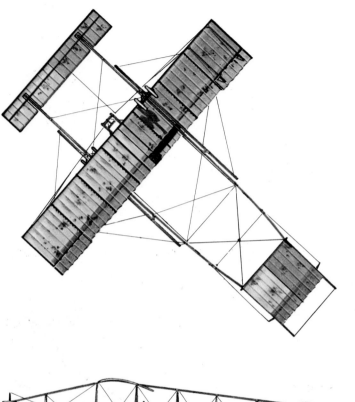

**12**

Henry Farman III, standard type, 1909. *Engine:* One 50 h.p. Gnome 7-cylinder rotary. *Span:* 32 ft. 9¾ in. (10·00 m.). *Length:* 39 ft. 4½ in. (12·00 m.). *Height:* approx. 11 ft. 6 in. (3·50 m.). *Wing area:* 430·56 sq. ft. (40·00 sq. m.). *Take-off weight:* 1,213 lb. (550 kg.). *Speed:* 37 m.p.h. (60 km./hr.). *Airframe:* ash and mahogany. *Propeller:* mahogany. *Covering:* unbleached cotton.

**13**

Bristol 'Boxkite' No. 12 of the Mission to India, January 1911. *Engine:* One 50 h.p. Gnome 7-cylinder rotary. *Span:* 46 ft. 6 in. (14·17 m.). *Length:* 38 ft. 6 in. (11·73 m.). *Height:* 11 ft. 10 in. (3·61 m.). *Wing area:* 517 sq. ft. (48·03 sq. m.). *Take-off weight:* 1,150 lb. (522 kg.). *Speed:* 40 m.p.h. (64 km./hr.). *Airframe:* ash and silver spruce. *Propeller:* mahogany. *Covering:* Zodiac rubberised fabric.

# GOLDEN FLYER (U.S.A.)

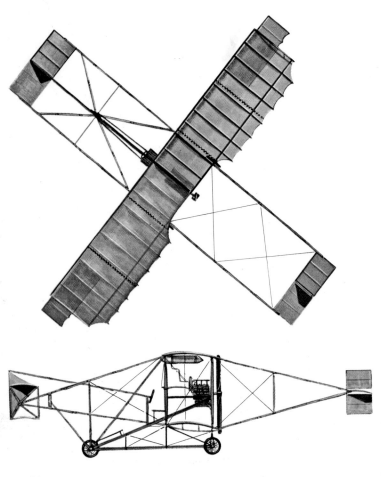

**14**

Curtiss Golden Flyer, autumn 1909. *Engine:* One 50 h.p. Curtiss 8-cylinder water-cooled Vee-type. *Span:* 28 ft. 9 in. (8·76 m.). *Span over ailerons:* 32 ft. 9 in. (9·98 m.). *Length:* 28 ft. 6 in. (8·69 m.). *Height:* approx. 9 ft. 0 in. (2·74 m.). *Wing area (including ailerons):* 258 sq. ft. (23·97 sq. m.). *Take-off weight:* 830 lb. (376 kg.). *Speed:* 45 m.p.h. (72 km./hr.). *Airframe:* Oregon spruce and bamboo. *Propeller:* spruce. *Covering:* Baldwin rubberised balloon silk.

## SILVER DART (U.S.A./Canada)

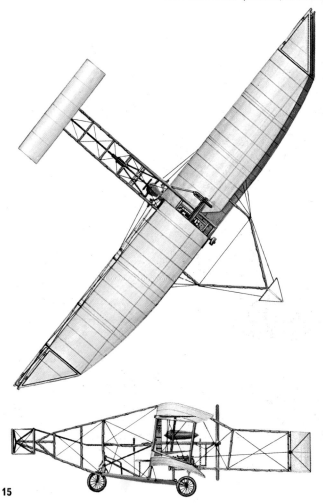

**15**

A.E.A. (McCurdy) *Silver Dart* as flown at Baddeck Bay, Nova Scotia, 23 February 1909. *Engine:* One 50 h.p. Curtiss 8-cylinder water-cooled Vee-type. *Span:* 49 ft. 1 in. (14·96 m.). *Length:* 32 ft. 1½ in. (9·79 m.). *Height:* 9 ft. 6 in. (2·90 m.). *Wing area:* 420 sq. ft. (39·02 sq. m.). *Take-off weight:* 860 lb. (390 kg.). *Speed:* approx. 40 m.p.h. (64 km./hr.). *Airframe:* bamboo, Oregon spruce and steel tube. *Propeller:* spruce. *Covering:* Baldwin rubberised silk.

# BRITISH ARMY AEROPLANE No. 1 (U.K.)

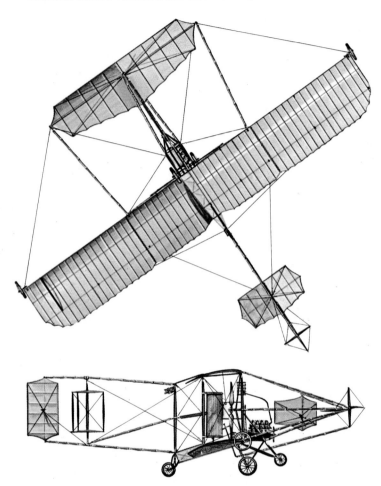

**16**

Cody British Army Aeroplane No. 1 at H.M. Balloon Factory, Farnborough, February 1909. *Engine:* One 50 h.p. Antoinette 8-cylinder water-cooled Vee-type. *Span:* 52 ft. 0 in. (15·85 m.). *Length:* 44 ft. 0 in. (13·41 m.). *Height:* 13 ft. 0 in. (3·96 m.). *Wing area:* 790 sq. ft. (73·39 sq. m.). *Take-off weight:* 2,540 lb. (1,152 kg.). *Speed:* 40 m.p.h. (64 km./hr.). *Airframe:* bamboo, pine and silver spruce. *Propellers:* steel shafts, aluminium blades. *Covering:* high grade, proofed kite silk (wings and tail); lightweight canvas (tailwheel support structure).

# CODY 1910 BIPLANE (U.K.)

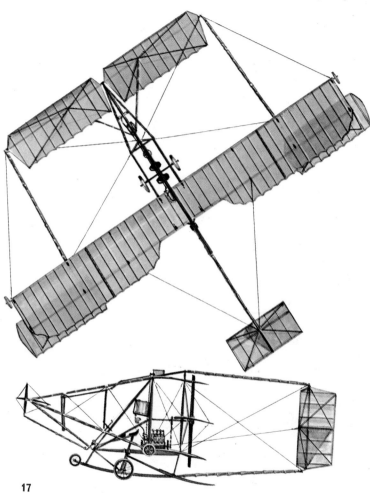

**17**

Cody Michelin Cup biplane, *ca.* November 1910. *Engine:* One 60 h.p. E.N.V.
Type F 8-cylinder water-cooled Vee-type. *Span:* 46 ft. 0 in. (14·02 m.). *Span:
over ailerons:* 49 ft. 0 in. (14·94 m.). *Length:* 38 ft. 6 in. (11·73 m.). *Height:*
13 ft. 0 in. (3·96 m.). *Wing area (including ailerons):* 640 sq. ft. (59·46 sq. m.).
*Take-off weight:* 2,950 lb. (1,338 kg.). *Speed:* 65 m.p.h. (105 km./hr.).
*Airframe:* silver spruce and bamboo. *Undercarriage:* steel tube and hickory.
*Propeller:* mahogany. *Covering:* Pegamoid oiled linen.

# PAULHAN BIPLANE (France)

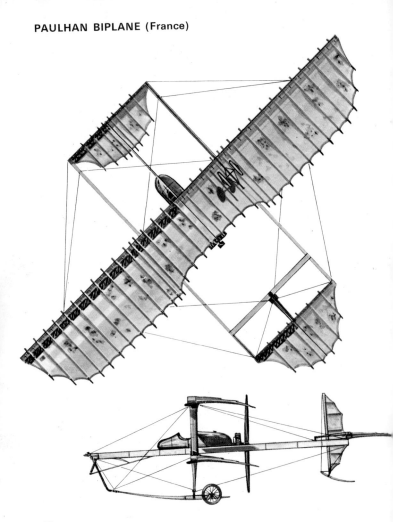

**18**

Paulhan biplane, as exhibited at the *Salon de l'Aeronautique*, Paris, October 1910. *Engine:* One 50 h.p. Gnome 7-cylinder rotary. *Span:* 40 ft. 0 in. (12·19 m.). *Length:* 28 ft. 2 in. (8·58 m.). *Height:* approx. 9 ft. 6 in. (2·90 m.). *Wing area:* approx. 215 sq. ft. (20·00 sq. m.). *Take-off weight:* 800 lb. (363 kg.). *Speed:* approx. 45 m.p.h. (72 km./hr.). *Airframe:* ash and spruce. *Propeller:* mahogany. *Covering:* aluminium (nacelle) and unbleached cotton (wings, tail and fuselage girders).

# MAYFLY (U.K.)

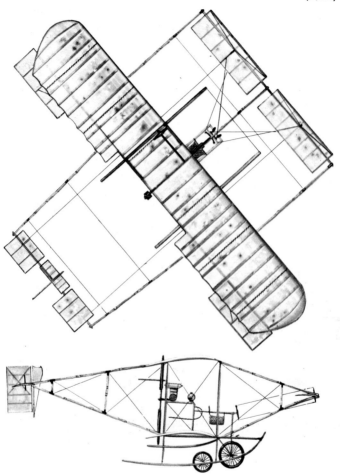

**19**

Bland Mayfly, *ca.* November/December 1910. *Engine:* One 20 h.p. Avro 2-cylinder horizontally opposed piston engine. *Span:* 27 ft. 7 in. (8·41 m.). *Length:* 23 ft. 0 in. (7·01 m.). *Height:* approx. 10 ft. 2 in. (3·10 m.). *Wing area:* 270 sq. ft. (25·08 sq. m.). *Take-off weight:* 526 lb. (239 kg.). *Airframe:* bamboo, American elm and ash. *Propeller:* mahogany. *Covering:* waterproofed unbleached calico.

## SHORT No. 3 (U.K.)

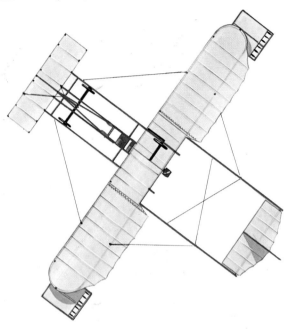

**20**

Short No. 3 biplane, *ca.* March 1910. *Engine:* One 35 h.p. Green 4-cylinder water-cooled in-line. *Span:* 31 ft. 8 in. (9·65 m.). *Span over ailerons:* 35 ft. 2 in. (10·72 m.). *Length:* 31 ft. 0 in. (9·45 m.). *Height:* approx. 8 ft. 8 in. (2·64 m.). *Wing area:* 282 sq. ft. (26·20 sq. m.). *Take-off weight:* 857 lb. (389 kg.). *Intended speed:* 45 m.p.h. (72 km./hr.). *Airframe:* spruce. *Propeller:* mahogany. *Covering:* North British rubberised cotton.

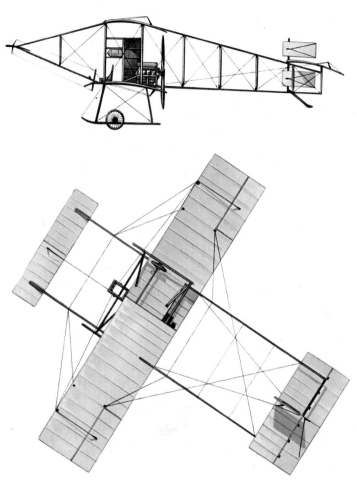

**21**

Short S.27 type, *ca.* June 1910. *Engine:* One 60 h.p. E.N.V. Type F 8-cylinder water-cooled Vee-type. *Span:* 34 ft. 2 in. (10·41 m.). *Length:* 40 ft. 6 in. (12·34 m.). *Height:* approx. 11 ft. 6 in. (3·50 m.). *Wing area:* 480 sq. ft. (44·59 sq. m.). *Take-off weight:* 1,400 lb. (635 kg.). *Speed:* 40 m.p.h. (64 km./hr.). *Airframe:* ash and spruce. *Propeller:* mahogany. *Covering:* unbleached cotton.

## FARMAN MF.7 (France)

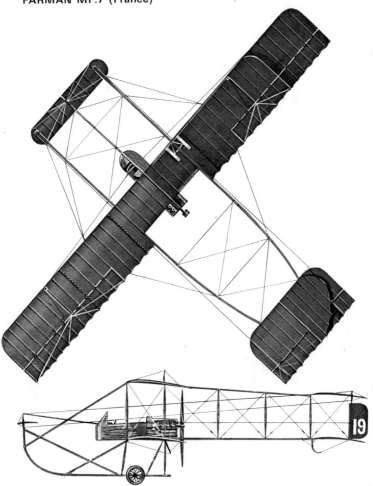

**22**

Maurice Farman MF.7 racer flown by Pierre Verrier in the first U.K. Aerial Derby at Hendon, June 1912. *Engine:* One 70 h.p. Renault 8-cylinder air-cooled Vee-type. *Span:* 51 ft. 8 in. (15·75 m.). *Length:* 39 ft. 6 in. (12·04 m.). *Height:* approx. 12 ft. 0 in. (3·66 m.). *Wing area:* 520 sq. ft. (48·31 sq. m.). *Take-off weight:* 1,606 lb. (728 kg.). *Speed:* 56 m.p.h. (90 km./hr.). *Airframe:* ash and mahogany. *Propeller:* mahogany. *Covering:* plywood (nacelle) and Continental rubberised fabric.

## FARMAN MF.11 (France)

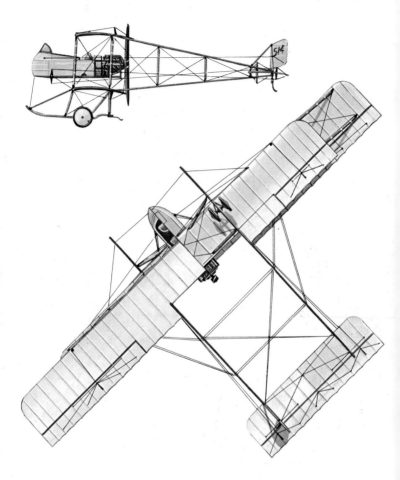

**23**

Maurice Farman-built MF.11 'Shorthorn' of the R.F.C. Military Wing, 1912.
*Engine:* One 70 h.p. Renault 8-cylinder air-cooled Vee-type. *Span:* 52 ft. 11$\frac{7}{8}$ in.
(16·20 m.). *Length:* 31 ft. 2$\frac{1}{8}$ in. (9·50 m.). *Height:* 10 ft. 6 in. (3·20 m.). *Wing
area:* 559·72 sq. ft. (52·00 sq. m.). *Take-off weight:* 2,039 lb. (925 kg.). *Speed:*
68 m.p.h. (110 km./hr.). *Airframe:* ash and spruce. *Propeller:* mahogany.
*Covering:* aluminium and plywood (nacelle), and unbleached cotton (wings
and tail).

# CHARABANC (U.K.)

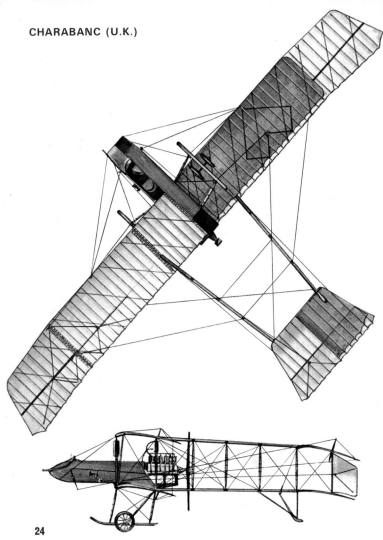

**24**

Grahame-White Type X Charabanc, 1913. *Engine:* One 90 or 120 h.p. Austro-Daimler 6-cylinder water-cooled in-line. *Span:* 62 ft. 0 in. (18·90 m.). *Length:* 37 ft. 6 in. (11·43 m.). *Height:* approx. 11 ft. 6 in. (3·51 m.). *Wing area:* 790 sq. ft. (73·39 sq. m.). *Take-off weight:* 3,100 lb. (1,406 kg.). *Speed:* 51 m.p.h. (82 km./hr.). *Airframe:* ash and spruce. *Propeller:* mahogany. *Covering:* plywood (nacelle) and lightweight proofed linen (wings and tail).

## FARMAN BIPLANE (France)

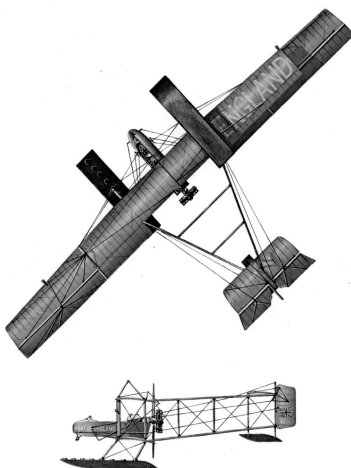

**25**

Henry Farman biplane flown by J. L. Travers with Claude Grahame-White during the 'Wake up, England!' campaign, July/August 1912. *Engine:* One 70 h.p. Gnome 7-cylinder rotary. *Span:* 50 ft. 11¼ in. (13·25 m.). *Length (land-plane):* 27 ft. 10⅝ in. (8·50 m.). *Length (floatplane):* approx. 28 ft. 6½ in. (8·70 m.). *Height:* 10 ft. 2 in. (3·10 m.). *Wing area:* 376·74 sq. ft. (35·00 sq. m.). *Take-off weight:* approx. 1,325 lb. (600 kg.). *Speed:* 50 m.p.h. (80 km./hr.). *Airframe:* spruce, ash and steel tube. *Propeller:* mahogany. *Covering:* aluminium and plywood (nacelle), mahogany ply and metal panels (floats), and bleached Egyptian cotton (wings and tail).

# WRIGHT BABY (U.S.A.)

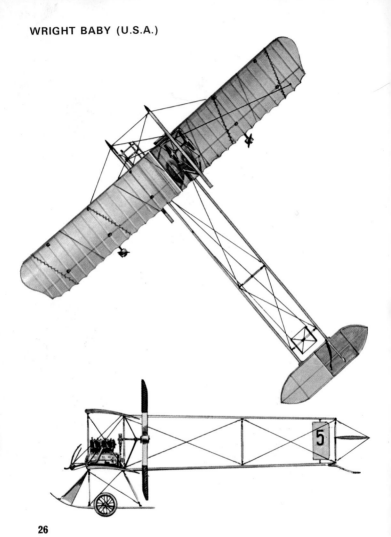

**26**

Wright Baby racer flown by W. R. Brookins in the Gordon Bennett Cup race, October 1910. *Engine:* One 60 h.p. Wright 8-cylinder water-cooled in-line. *Span:* 21 ft. 5 in. (6·53 m.). *Length:* 19 ft. 6 in. (5·94 m.). *Height:* 6 ft. 10 in. (2·08 m.). *Wing area:* 145 sq. ft. (13·47 sq. m.). *Take-off weight:* 860 lb. (390 kg.). *Speed:* approx. 75 m.p.h. (121 km./hr.). *Airframe:* ash and spruce. *Propellers:* yellow pine. *Covering:* bleached cotton.

**27**

Royal Aircraft Factory F.E.3, *ca.* summer 1913. *Engine:* One 100 h.p. Chenu 6-cylinder water-cooled in-line. *Span:* 41 ft. 3 in. (12·57 m.). *Length:* 29 ft. 8 in. (9·04 m.). *Height:* 11 ft. 3 in. (3·43 m.). *Wing area:* 436·5 sq. ft. (40·55 sq. m.). *Take-off weight:* 2,080 lb. (943 kg.). *Speed:* 75 m.p.h. (121 km./hr.). *Airframe:* steel tube and spruce. *Propeller:* laminated mahogany. *Covering:* aluminium (nacelle) and lightweight linen (wings and tail).

# DUNNE D.5 (U.K.)

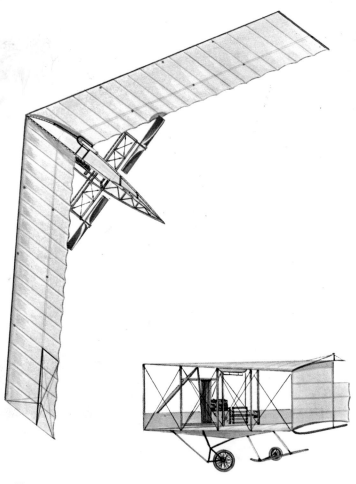

**28**

Dunne D. 5, *ca.* summer 1910. *Engine:* One 60 h.p. Green 4-cylinder water-cooled in-line. *Span:* 46 ft. 0 in. (14·02 m.). *Length overall:* 20 ft. 4½ in. (6·21 m.). *Length of nacelle:* 18 ft. 0 in. (5·49 m.). *Height:* approx. 11 ft. 6 in. (3·51 m.). *Wing area:* 527 sq. ft. (48·96 sq. m.). *Take-off weight:* 1,550 lb. (703 kg.). *Speed:* approx. 45 m.p.h. (72 km./hr.). *Airframe:* ash, spruce, pine and steel tube. *Propellers:* mahogany. *Covering:* bleached linen.

# DUNNE D.8 (U.K.)

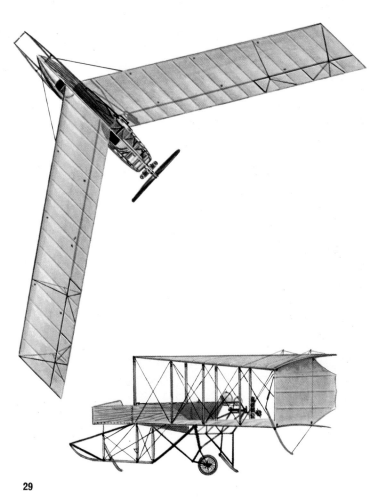

**29**

Dunne D.8, *ca.* autumn 1913. *Engine:* One 80 h.p. Gnome 7-cylinder rotary. *Span:* 46 ft. 0 in. (14·02 m.). *Length overall:* approx. 26 ft. 6 in. (8·08 m.). *Length of nacelle:* approx. 15 ft. 6 in. (4·72 m.). *Height:* approx. 13 ft. 0 in. (3·96 m.). *Wing area:* 545 sq. ft. (50·63 sq. m.). *Take-off weight:* 1,900 lb. (862 kg.). *Speed:* 55 m.p.h. (88·5 km./hr.). *Airframe:* ash, spruce, pine and steel tube. *Propeller:* mahogany. *Covering:* thin plywood sheet (nacelle) and unbleached linen (wings).

# BURGESS-DUNNE AH-7 (U.S.A.)

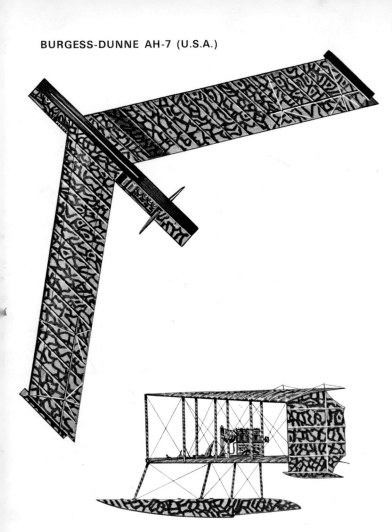

**30**

Burgess-Dunne AH-7 of the U.S. Navy, *ca*. December 1914. *Engine:* One 90 h.p. Curtiss 8-cylinder water-cooled Vee-type. *Span:* 47 ft. 0 in. (14·33 m.). *Length:* approx. 24 ft. 0 in. (7·32 m.). *Height:* 11 ft. 0 in. (3·35 m.). *Wing area:* 482 sq. ft. (44·78 sq. m.). *Take-off weight:* approx. 2,150 lb. (975 kg.). *Speed:* 75 m.p.h. (121 km./hr.). *Airframe:* spruce, pine and steel tube. *Propeller:* mahogany. Covering: plywood sheet (floats) and unbleached linen (wings and vertical surfaces).

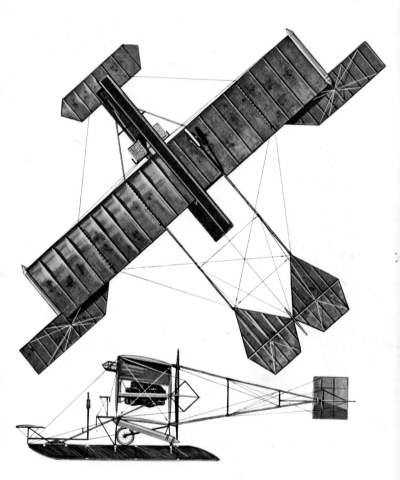

**31**

Curtiss seaplane A. 1 of the U.S. Navy, *ca.* January/February 1911. *Engine:* One 75 h.p. Curtiss Model O 8-cylinder water-cooled Vee-type. *Span:* 28 ft. 8 in. (8·74 m.). *Span over ailerons:* 37 ft. 0 in. (11·28 m.). *Length:* 27 ft. 8 in. (8·43 m.). *Height:* 9 ft. 4 in. (2·84 m.). *Wing area (including ailerons):* 331 sq. ft. (30·75 sq. m.). *Take-off weight:* 1,575 lb. (714 kg.). *Speed:* approx. 65 m.p.h. (105 km./hr.). *Airframe:* Oregon spruce, bamboo and steel tube. *Propeller:* laminated mahogany. *Covering:* mahogany ply (float-hull) with ash rubbing strakes; proofed, rubberised fabric (wings and tail).

# CURTISS FLYING BOAT (U.S.A.)

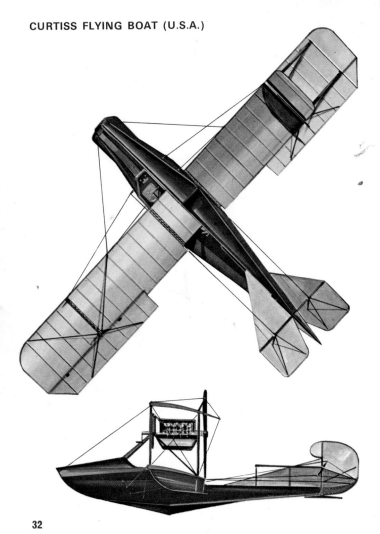

**32**

Curtiss flying boat, spring 1914. *Engine:* One 100 h.p. Curtiss OX 8-cylinder water-cooled Vee-type. *Span:* 41 ft. 0 in. (12·50 m.). *Length:* 27 ft. 4 in. (8·33 m.). *Height:* approx. 11 ft. 0 in. (3·35 m.). *Wing area:* 378 sq. ft. (35·12 sq. m.). *Take-off weight:* 1,760 lb. (798 kg.). *Speed:* approx. 65 m.p.h. (105 km./hr.). *Airframe:* spruce and pine. *Propeller:* laminated mahogany. *Covering:* mahogany (hull) and bleached linen (wings and tail).

# DONNET-LÉVÊQUE TYPE A (France)

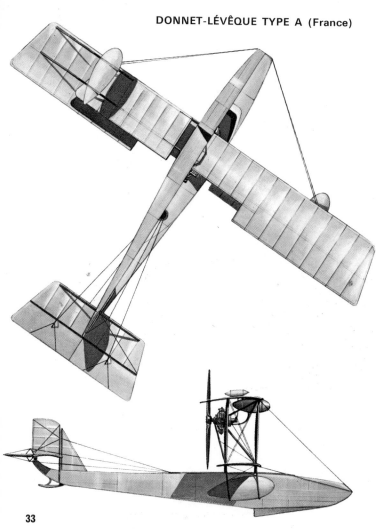

**33**

Donnet-Lévêque Type A flying boat, L.1 of the Royal Swedish Navy, 1913. *Engine:* One 50 h.p. Gnome 7-cylinder rotary. *Span:* 31 ft. 2 in. (9·50 m.). *Length:* 27 ft. 10⅝ in. (8·50 m.). *Height:* approx. 11 ft. 1⅞ in. (3·40 m.). *Wing area:* 183 sq. ft. (17·00 sq. m.). *Take-off weight:* approx. 1,323 lb. (600 kg.). *Speed:* 68 m.p.h. (110 km./hr.). *Airframe:* spruce and pine. *Propeller:* mahogany. *Covering:* mahogany ply (hull) and Pegamoid-type oiled linen (wings and tail).

# BAT BOAT (U.K.)

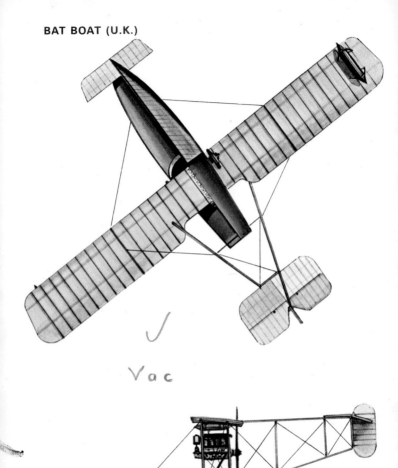

**34**

Sopwith Bat Boat, early summer 1913. *Engine:* One 90 h.p. Austro-Daimler water-cooled in-line. *Span:* 41 ft. 0 in. (12·50 m.). *Length:* 30 ft. 4 in. (9·24 m.). *Height:* 11 ft. 6 in. (3·50 m.). *Wing area:* 428 sq. ft. (39·76 sq. m.). *Take-off weight:* 1,700 lb. (771 kg.). *Speed:* 65 m.p.h. (105 km./hr.). *Airframe:* ash. *Propeller:* mahogany. *Covering:* cedar planking (hull) and unbleached linen (wings and tail).

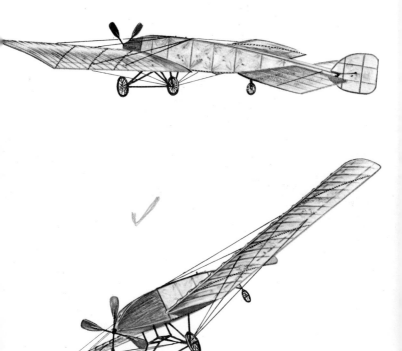

**35**

Blériot VII monoplane, *ca.* December 1907. *Engine:* One 50 h.p. Antoinette 8-cylinder water-cooled Vee-type. *Span:* 36 ft. 1⅛ in. (11·00 m.). *Length:* approx. 26 ft. 3 in. (8·00 m.). *Height:* approx. 9 ft. 0 in. (2·75 m.). *Wing area:* 269·10 sq. ft. (25·00 sq. m.). *Take-off weight:* 937 lb. (425 kg.). *Speed:* 50 m.p.h. (80 km./hr.). *Airframe:* ash, spruce and steel tube. *Propeller:* steel shafts, aluminium blades. *Covering:* aluminium and plywood (engine and front of fuselage); bleached cotton and/or varnished paper (wings, tail and rear of fuselage).

## DEMOISELLE (Brazil/France)

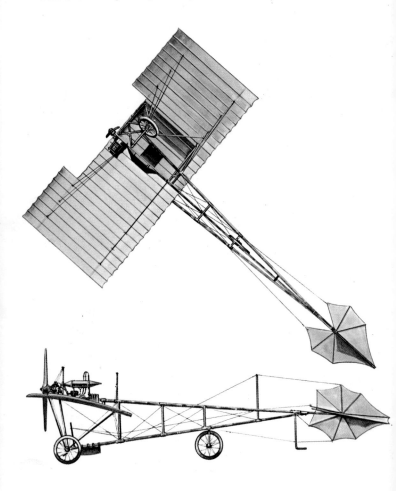

**36**

Santos-Dumont No. 20 Demoiselle, spring/summer 1909. *Engine:* One 35 h.p. Darracq-built Dutheil-Chalmers 2-cylinder horizontally opposed piston engine. *Span:* 16 ft. 8¾ in. (5·10 m.). *Length:* 26 ft. 3 in. (8·00 m.). *Height:* 7 ft. 10½ in. (2·40 m.). *Wing area:* 110 sq. ft. (10·20 sq. m.). *Take-off weight:* 315 lb. (143 kg.). *Speed:* 56 m.p.h. (90 km./hr.). *Airframe:* bamboo and steel tube. *Propeller:* mahogany. *Covering:* Japanese silk.

# BLACKBURN 1909 MONOPLANE (U.K.)

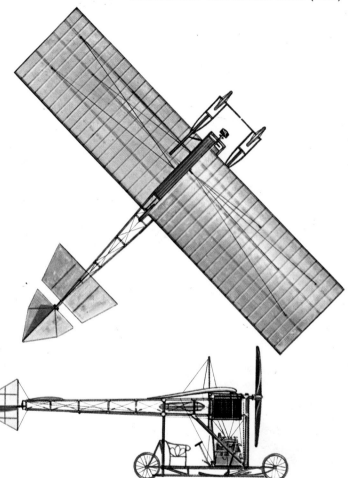

**37**

Blackburn 'heavy' monoplane, *ca.* summer 1909. *Engine:* One 35 h.p. Green 4-cylinder water-cooled in-line. *Span:* 30 ft. 0 in. (9·14 m.). *Length:* 26 ft. 0 in. (7·92 m.). *Height:* approx. 9 ft. 6 in. (2·90 m.). *Wing area:* 170 sq. ft. (15·79 sq. m.). *Empty weight:* 800 lb. (363 kg.). *Speed:* 60 m.p.h. (97 km./hr.). *Airframe:* spruce, ash and steel tube. *Propeller:* walnut. *Covering:* unbleached cotton.

53

# VUIA No. 1 (Rumania/France)

**38**

Vuia No. 1 monoplane, 1906. *Engine:* One 25 h.p. Serpollet carbonic acid gas engine. *Span:* 28 ft. 6½ in. (8·70 m.). *Length:* 9 ft. 10⅛ in. (3·00 m.). *Height:* approx. 10 ft. 9 in. (3·28 m.). *Wing area:* 215·3 sq. ft. (20·00 sq. m.). *Take-off weight:* 531 lb. (241 kg.). *Airframe:* steel tube. *Propeller:* fabric-covered. *Covering:* unbleached cotton or muslin.

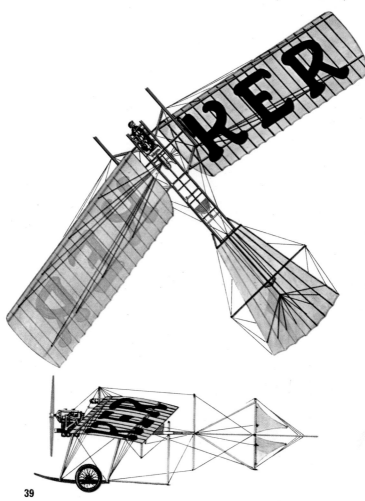

**39**

Fokker A-1912 *Spin* (Spider), *ca.* spring 1912. *Engine:* One 50 h.p. Argus 4-cylinder water-cooled in-line. *Span:* 36 ft. 1 in. (11·00 m.). *Length:* 25 ft. 5⅛ in. (7·75 m.). *Height:* 9 ft. 10⅛ in. (3·00 m.). *Wing area:* 236·81 sq. ft. (22·00 sq. m.). *Take-off weight:* 882 lb. (400 kg.). *Maximum speed:* 56 m.p.h. (90 km./hr.). *Airframe:* steel tube, ash and bamboo. *Propeller:* laminated mahogany. *Covering:* bleached cotton.

## TAUBE (Austria)

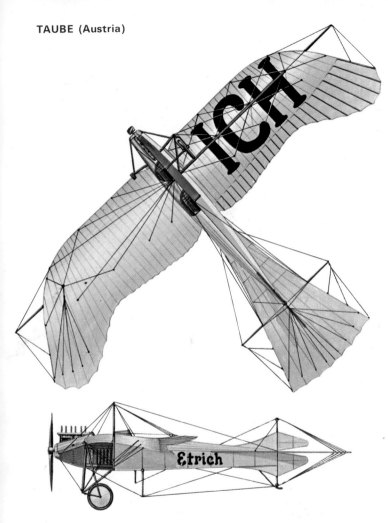

**40**

Etrich *Taube, ca.* 1912. *Engine:* One 100/120 h.p. Mercedes 6-cylinder water-cooled in-line. *Span:* 47 ft. 1 in. (14·35 m.). *Length:* 32 ft. 3¾ in. (9·85 m.). *Height:* 10 ft. 4⅛ in. (3·15 m.). *Wing area:* approx. 375 sq. ft. (34·84 sq. m.). *Take-off weight:* 1,918 lb. (870 kg.). *Maximum speed:* 71·5 m.p.h. (115 km./hr.) at sea level. *Airframe:* spruce and steel tube. *Propeller:* mahogany. *Covering:* aluminium and varnished plywood (engine and cockpit decking); unbleached cotton (wings, tail and rear of fuselage).

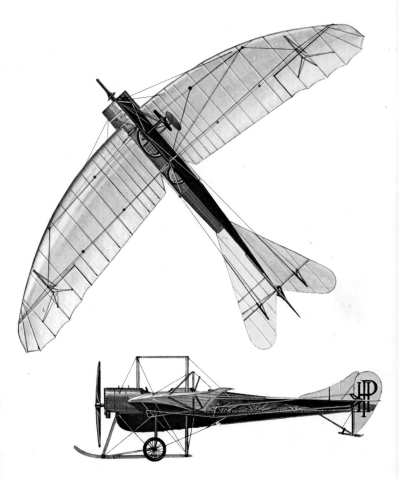

**41**

Modified Handley Page Type E ('Yellow Peril'), *ca.* April/May 1913. *Engine:* One 50 h.p. Gnome 7-cylinder rotary. *Span:* 42 ft. 3 in. (12·88 m.). *Length:* 28 ft. 2 in. (8·59 m.). *Height:* 9 ft. 4 in. (2·84 m.). *Wing area:* 240 sq. ft. (22·30 sq. m.). *Take-off weight:* 1,300 lb. (590 kg.). *Speed:* 60 m.p.h. (97 km./hr.). *Airframe:* ash. *Propeller:* mahogany. *Covering:* aluminium and thin mahogany plywood (fuselage); cellulose-coated bleached cotton (wings and tail).

# ANTOINETTE VII (France)

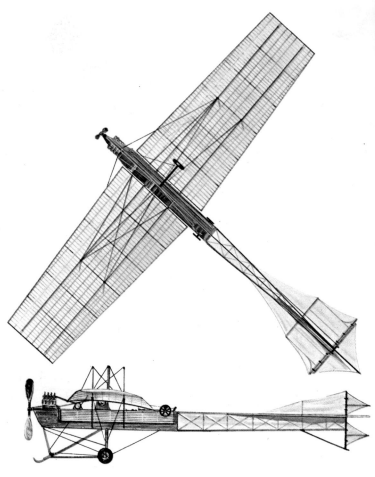

**42**

Antoinette VII monoplane, 1909. *Engine:* One 50 h.p. Antoinette 8-cylinder water-cooled Vee-type. *Span:* 42 ft. 0 in. (12·80 m.). *Length:* 37 ft. 8¾ in. (11·50 m.). *Height:* 9 ft. 10 in. (3·00 m.). *Wing area:* 538·20 sq. ft. (50·00 sq. m.). *Take-off weight:* 1,301 lb. (590 kg.). *Maximum speed:* 43·5 m.p.h. (70 km./hr.). *Airframe:* ash and spruce. *Propeller:* steel shafts, aluminium blades. *Covering:* cedar panels (front of fuselage) and Michelin rubberised fabric (wings, tail and rear of fuselage).

# MARTIN-HANDASYDE MONOPLANE (U.K.)

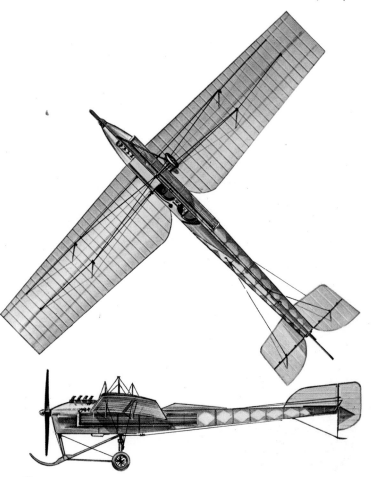

**43**

Martin-Handasyde monoplane ('the magnificent Martinsyde') flown by Bell,
Gilmour and Sopwith at Brooklands, *ca.* January 1912. *Engine:* One 65 h.p.
Antoinette 8-cylinder water-cooled Vee-type. *All other data estimated. Span:*
40 ft. 0 in. (12·19 m.). *Length:* 35 ft. 0 in. (10·67 m.). *Height:* 9 ft. 3 in. (2·82 m.).
*Wing area:* 250 sq. ft. (23·23 sq. m.). *Take-off weight:* 1,500 lb. (680 kg.).
*Speed:* 60 m.p.h. (97 km./hr.). *Airframe:* ash, spruce and steel tube; fuselage
reinforcing panels of plywood with diamond-shaped cut-outs. *Propeller:*
mahogany. *Covering:* aluminium (cowling) and plywood (cockpit decking and
centre of fuselage); bleached linen (wings, tail and rear of fuselage).

## FLANDERS F.3 (U.K.)

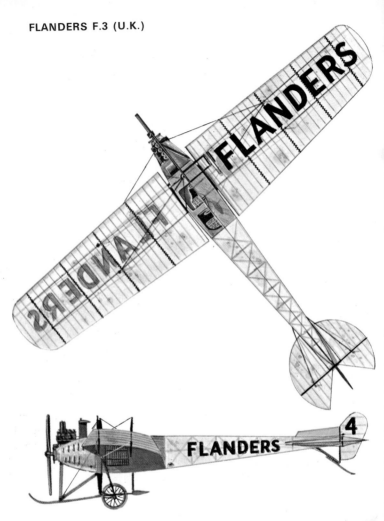

**44**

Flanders F.3 flown by E.V.B. Fisher at Brooklands *ca.* March/April 1912. *Engine:* One 60 h.p. Green 4-cylinder water-cooled in-line. *Span:* 42 ft. 0 in. (12·80 m.). *Length:* 31 ft. 9 in. (9·68 m.). *Height:* 9 ft. 3 in. (2·82 m.). *Wing area:* 240 sq. ft. (22·30 sq. m.). *Take-off weight:* approx. 1,600 lb. (726 kg.). *Speed:* 65 m.p.h. (105 km./hr.). *Airframe:* ash, spruce and steel tube and strip. *Propeller:* mahogany. *Covering:* aluminium (cowling), plywood sheet (centre of fuselage) and unbleached linen (wings, tail and rear of fuselage).

# HANRIOT MONOPLANE (France)

**45**

Hanriot monoplane flown by Marcel Hanriot, *ca.* autumn 1910. *Engine:* One 35 h.p. E.N.V. Type D 8-cylinder water-cooled Vee-type. *Span:* 30 ft. 0¼ in. (9·15 m.). *Length:* 27 ft. 0¾ in. (8·25 m.). *Height:* 7 ft. 0⅝ in. (2·15 m.). *Wing area:* 182·99 sq. ft. (17·00 sq. m.). *Take-off weight:* approx. 500 lb. (227 kg.). *Airframe:* ash, spruce and steel tube. *Propeller:* mahogany. *Covering:* mahogany ply (fuselage) and unbleached cotton (wings and tail).

## BLERIOT XI (France)

**46**

The modified Type XI in which Louis Blériot made the first aeroplane crossing of the English Channel, 25 July 1909. *Engine:* One 25 h.p. Anzani 3-cylinder air-cooled semi-radial. *Span:* 25 ft. 7⅛ in. (7·80 m.). *Length:* 26 ft. 3 in. (8·00 m.). *Height:* approx. 8 ft. 6⅜ in. (2·60 m.). *Wing area:* 150·70 sq. ft. (14·00 sq. m.). *Take-off weight:* 661 lb. (300 kg.). *Speed:* approx. 47 m.p.h. (75 km./hr.). *Airframe:* steel tube, ash and bamboo. *Propeller:* laminated walnut. *Covering:* Continental rubberised and waterproofed fabric. Inflatable rubberised air bag within fuselage frame during Channel flight.

# BLACKBURN 1912 MONOPLANE (U.K.)

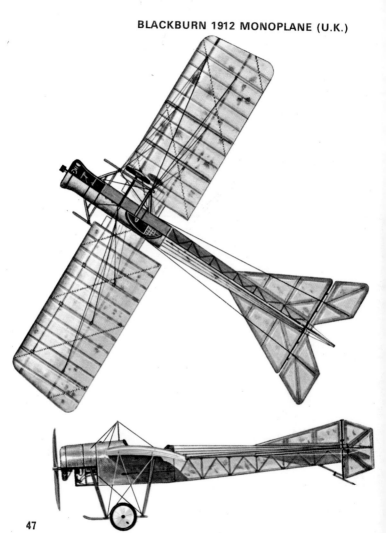

47

Blackburn single-seat monoplane built for Cyril Foggin, *ca.* January/February 1913. *Engine:* One 50 h.p. Gnome 7-cylinder rotary. *Span:* 35 ft. 8 in. (10·87 m.). *Length:* 26 ft. 3 in. (8·00 m.). *Height:* 8 ft. 9 in. (2·67 m.). *Wing area:* 236 sq. ft. (21·93 sq. m.). *Take-off weight:* 800 lb. (363 kg.). *Speed:* 60 m.p.h. (97 km./hr.). *Airframe:* ash and spruce. *Propeller:* mahogany. *Covering:* clear-doped cotton.

## R.E.P. 2bis (France)

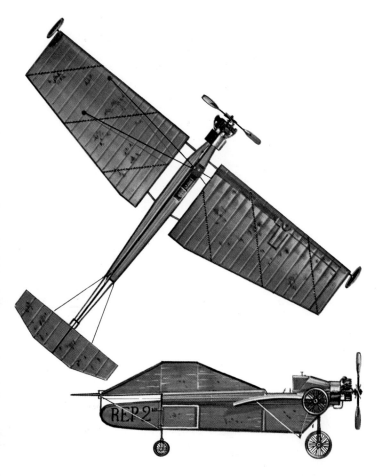

**48**

Esnault-Pelterie R.E.P. 2*bis* as modified, probably for the Rheims meeting of August 1909. *Engine:* One 30 h.p. R.E.P. 7-cylinder air-cooled semi-radial. *Span:* 28 ft. 2⅝ in. (8·60 m.). *Length:* approx. 22 ft. 6¾ in. (6·85 m.). *Height:* approx. 8 ft. 2½ in. (2·50 m.). *Wing area:* 169·5 sq. ft. (15·75 sq. m.). *Take-off weight:* 772 lb. (350 kg.). *Speed:* approx. 50 m.p.h. (80 km./hr.). *Airframe:* steel tube and aluminium. *Propeller:* steel shafts, aluminium blades. *Covering:* aluminium (engine cowling) and proofed balloon silk.

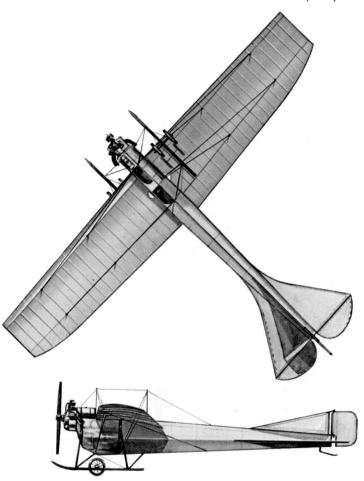

**49**

Vickers No. 1 monoplane, July 1911. *Engine:* One 60 h.p. R.E.P. 5-cylinder air-cooled semi-radial. *Span:* 47 ft. 6 in. (14·48 m.). *Length:* 36 ft. 5 in. (11·10 m.). *Height:* 9 ft. 7 in. (2·92 m.). *Wing area:* 290 sq. ft. (26·94 m.). *Take-off weight:* approx. 1,150 lb. (522 kg.). *Speed:* 56 m.p.h. (90 km./hr.). *Airframe:* steel tube and ash. *Propeller:* mahogany. *Covering:* aluminium (engine and cockpit decking) and bleached cotton (wings, tail and rear of fuselage).

# AVRO TYPE F (U.K.)

**50**

Avro Type F, summer 1912. *Engine:* One 35 h.p. Viale 5-cylinder air-cooled radial. *Span:* 29 ft. 0 in. (8·84 m.). *Length:* 23 ft. 0 in. (7·01 m.). *Height:* approx. 7 ft. 6 in. (2·29 m.). *Wing area:* 158 sq. ft. (14·68 sq. m.). *Take-off weight:* 800 lb. (363 kg.). *Speed:* 65 m.p.h. (105 km./hr.). *Airframe:* ash, spruce and steel tube. *Propeller:* mahogany. *Covering:* aluminium (front of fuselage) and unbleached linen (wings, tail and rear of fuselage).

# DEPERDUSSIN TYPE B (France)

**51**

Deperdussin Type B military single-seater, 1911. *Engine:* One 50 h.p. Gnome 7-cylinder rotary. *Span:* 28 ft. 10½ in. (8·80 m.). *Length:* 24 ft. 11¼ in. (7·60 m.). *Height:* approx. 8 ft. 2½ in. (2·50 m.). *Wing area:* 263·72 sq. ft. (24·50 sq. m.). *Take-off weight:* 551 lb. (250 kg.). *Speed:* 65 m.p.h. (105 km./hr.). *Airframe:* ash and spruce. *Propeller:* mahogany. *Covering:* aluminium (cowling), plywood (cockpit floor and ventral fairing) and oiled cotton (fuselage, wings and tail).

# BRISTOL (PRIER) MONOPLANE (U.K.)

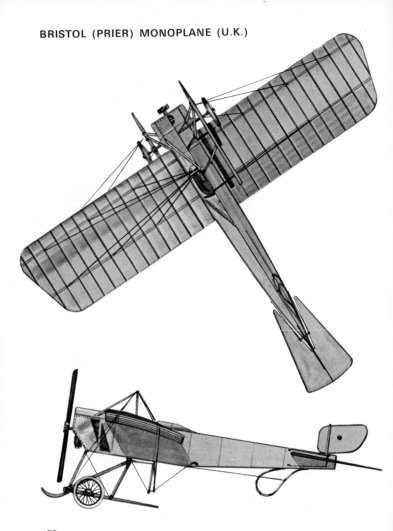

**52**

Bristol (Prier) P-1 No. 56, owned by James Valentine, *ca.* September 1911.
*Engine:* One 50 h.p. Gnome 7-cylinder rotary. *Span:* 30 ft. 2 in. (9·19 m.).
*Length:* 24 ft. 6 in. (7·47 m.). *Height:* 9 ft. 9 in. (2·97 m.). *Wing area:* 166 sq. ft.
(15·42 sq. m.). *Take-off weight:* 820 lb. (372 kg.). *Speed:* 68 m.p.h. (109
km./hr.). *Airframe:* ash and steel tube. *Propeller:* mahogany. *Covering:* aluminium
(front of fuselage) and Zodiac rubberised fabric (wings, tail and rear of fuselage).

# BRISTOL (COANDA) MONOPLANE (U.K.)

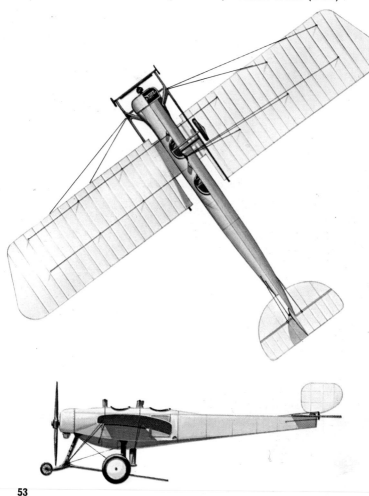

53

Bristol (Coanda) military monoplane No. 153, exhibited at Olympia Aero Show, February 1913. *Engine:* One 80 h.p. Gnome 7-cylinder rotary. *Span:* 42 ft. 8 in. (13·00 m.). *Length:* 29 ft. 2 in. (8·89 m.). *Height:* 7 ft. 0 in. (2·13 m.). *Wing area:* 280 sq. ft. (26·01 sq. m.). *Take-off weight:* 1,775 lb. (805 kg.). *Speed:* 71 m.p.h. (114 km./hr.). *Airframe:* spruce, ash and steel tube. *Propeller:* mahogany. *Covering:* aluminium (front of fuselage), birch ply (top decking) and unbleached cotton (wings and tail).

## NIEUPORT MONOPLANE (France)

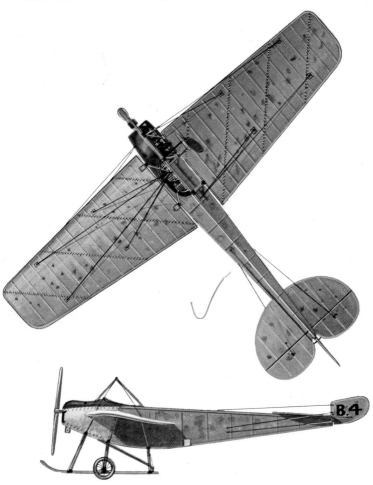

**54**

Nieuport 2-seat monoplane of the Air Battalion, Royal Engineers, flown by Lt. Barrington-Kennett in the competition for the Mortimer Singer prize, 14 February 1912. *Engine:* One 50 h.p. Gnome 7-cylinder rotary. *Span:* 36 ft. 1⅛ in. (11·00 m.). *Length:* 27 ft. 6¾ in. (8·40 m.). *Height:* 8 ft. 6⅜ in. (2·60 m.). *Wing area:* 226·04 sq. ft. (21·00 sq. m.). *Take-off weight:* 717 lb. (325 kg.). *Speed:* 55 m.p.h. (88 km./hr.). *Airframe:* spruce, ash and steel tube. *Propeller:* mahogany. *Covering:* aluminium (cowling) and proofed linen (fuselage, wings and tail).

## NIEUPORT IVG (France)

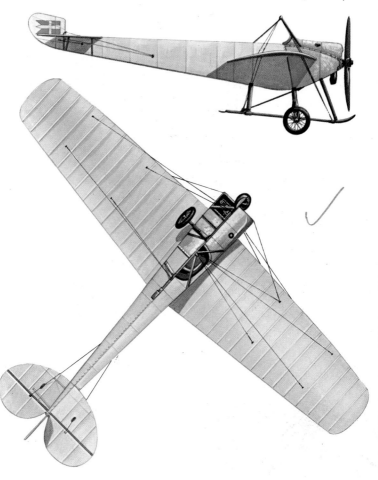

**55**

Nieuport IVG of the Royal Swedish Army Air Division, 1912. *Engine:* One 50 h.p. Gnome 7-cylinder rotary. *Span:* 38 ft. 0⅞ in. (11·60 m.). *Length:* 25 ft. 7⅛ in. (7·80 m.). *Height:* 8 ft. 2⅜ in. (2·50 m.). *Wing area:* approx. 188·37 sq. ft. (17·50 sq. m.). *Empty weight:* 772 lb. (350 kg.). *Speed:* 65 m.p.h. (105 km./hr.). *Airframe:* spruce and steel tube. *Propeller:* laminated mahogany. *Covering:* proofed linen.

# MORANE-SAULNIER TYPE G (France)

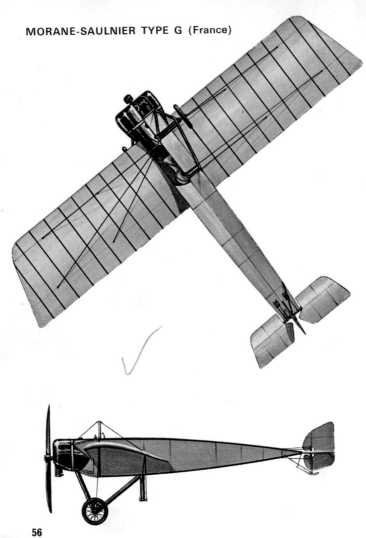

**56**

Morane-Saulnier Type G owned by M. Robert Morane, 1913; now exhibited in the *Musee de l'Air*, Paris. *Engine:* One 80 h.p. Gnome 7-cylinder rotary. *Span:* 30 ft. 6⅛ in. (9·30 m.). *Length:* 21 ft. 5⅞ in. (6·55 m.). *Height:* approx. 9 ft. 0 in. (2·75 m.). *Wing area:* 160 sq. ft. (14·86 sq. m.). *Take-off weight:* approx. 816 lb. (370 kg.). *Speed:* 80 m.p.h. (129 km./hr.). *Airframe:* spruce and flattened steel tube; wooden wheels. *Propeller:* mahogany. *Covering:* plywood (front of fuselage) and proofed linen (wings, tail and rear of fuselage).

# DEPERDUSSIN RACER (France)

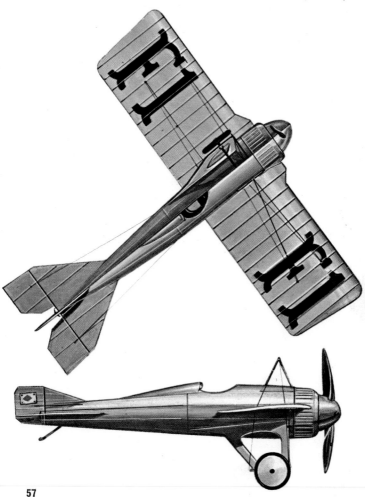

**57**

Deperdussin 'monocoque' racer, 1913. *Engine:* One 160 h.p. Gnome 14-cylinder two-row rotary. *Span:* 21 ft. 9¾ in. (6·65 m.). *Length:* 20 ft. 0⅛ in. (6·10 m.). *Height:* approx. 7 ft. 6½ in. (2·30 m.). *Wing area:* 104 sq. ft. (9·66 sq. m.). *Take-off weight:* 992 lb. (450 kg.). *Speed:* 127 m.p.h. (204 km./hr.). *Airframe:* ash. *Propeller:* mahogany. *Covering:* plywood (fuselage); proofed linen (wings and tail).

# ANTOINETTE LATHAM (France)

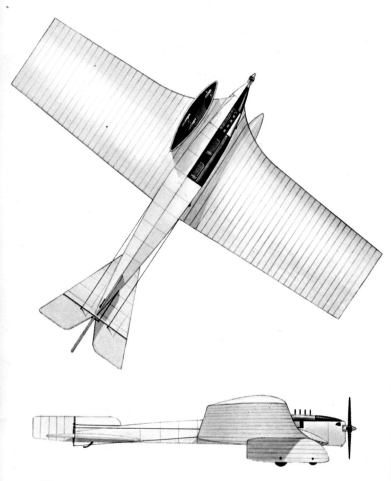

**58**

Antoinette *Type Latham* (or *Monobloc*), summer 1911. *Engine:* One 50 h.p.
Antoinette 8-cylinder water-cooled Vee-type. *Span:* 52 ft. 2 in. (15·90 m.).
*Length:* 37 ft. 8¾ in. (11·50 m.). *Height:* approx. 8 ft. 2½ in. (2·50 m.). *Wing
area:* 602·78 sq. ft. (56·00 sq. m.). *Take-off weight:* 2,976 lb. (1,350 kg.).
*Airframe:* ash and steel tube. *Propeller:* mahogany. *Covering:* aluminium and
proofed linen.

## CAUDRON TYPE A (France)

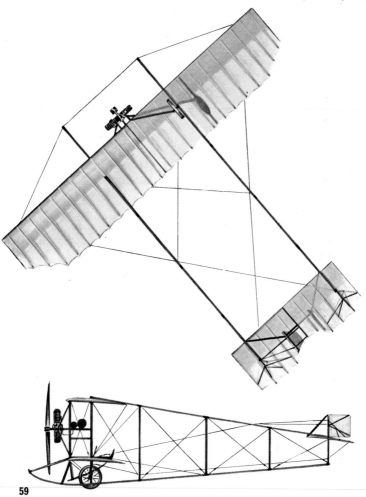

**59**

Caudron Type A prototype flown at Issy-les-Moulineaux by Céi, March 1911. *Engine:* One 45 h.p. Anzani 5-cylinder air-cooled semi-radial. *Span:* 26 ft. 3 in. (8·00 m.). *Length:* 26 ft. 3 in. (8·00 m.). *Height:* approx. 9 ft. 0 in. (2·75 m.). *Wing area:* 236·80 sq. ft. (22·00 sq. m.). *Take-off weight:* approx. 595 lb. (270 kg.). *Speed:* 53 m.p.h. (85 km./hr.). *Airframe:* spruce and ash. *Propeller:* laminated mahogany. *Covering:* bleached cotton.

## TRIPLE TWIN (U.K.)

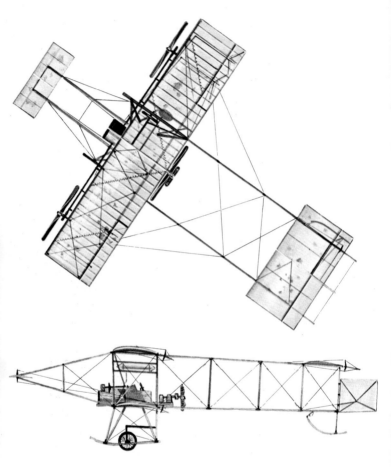

**60**

Short Triple Twin built for Francis McClean, 1911. *Engines:* Two 50 h.p. Gnome 7-cylinder rotaries. *Span:* 34 ft. 0 in. (10·36 m.). *Length:* 45 ft. 0 in. (13·72 m.). *Height:* 12 ft. 0 in. (3·66 m.). *Wing area:* 435 sq. ft. (40·41 sq. m.). *Take-off weight:* 2,100 lb. (952 kg.). *Speed:* 55 m.p.h. (89 km./hr.). *Airframe:* ash and spruce. *Propellers:* mahogany. *Covering:* aluminium (cowling), plywood (rear of nacelle) and unbleached cotton (wings and tail).

## GOUPY III (France)

**61**

Goupy III of the Goupy School, Juvisy, *ca.* October 1910. *Engine:* One 30 h.p.
Anzani 3-cylinder air-cooled semi-radial. *Span:* 20 ft. 4⅛ in. (6·20 m.). *Length:*
24 ft. 7¼ in. (7·50 m.). *Height:* approx. 8 ft. 2½ in. (2·50 m.). *Wing area:*
215·28 sq. ft. (20·00 sq. m.). *Loaded weight (without pilot):* 595 lb. (270 kg.).
*Speed:* approx. 60 m.p.h. (97 km./hr.). *Airframe:* ash and spruce. *Propeller:*
mahogany. *Covering:* unbleached cotton.

# AVRO TYPE E (U.K.)

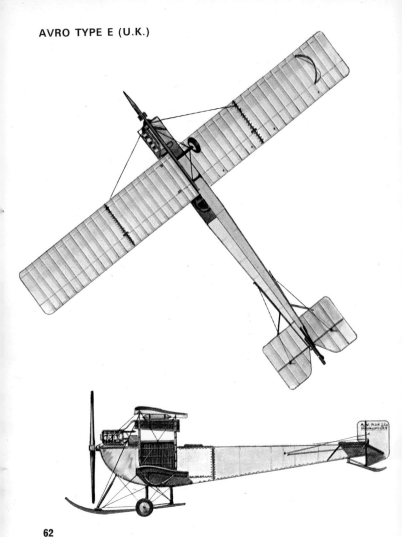

**62**

Prototype Avro Type E, *ca.* March 1912. *Engine:* One 60 h.p. E.N.V. Type F 8-cylinder water-cooled Vee-type. *Span:* 36 ft. 0 in. (10·97 m.). *Length:* 30 ft. 6 in. (9·30 m.). *Height:* 9 ft. 9 in. (3·12 m.). *Wing area:* 330 sq. ft. (30·66 sq. m.). *Take-off weight:* 1,650 lb. (748 kg.). *Speed:* 50 m.p.h. (80 km./hr.). *Airframe:* ash, spruce and steel tube. *Propeller:* mahogany. *Covering:* aluminium (front of fuselage), plywood (cockpit decking), canvas (centre of fuselage) and unbleached linen (wings, tail and rear of fuselage).

**63**

Avro Type G flown in the Military Trials at Larkhill, August 1912. *Engine:* One 60 h.p. Green 4-cylinder water-cooled in-line. *Span:* 35 ft. 3 in. (10·74 m.). *Length:* 28 ft. 6 in. (8·69 m.). *Height:* 9 ft. 9 in. (2·97 m.). *Wing area:* 310 sq. ft. (28·80 sq. m.). *Take-off weight:* 1,792 lb. (813 kg.). *Maximum speed:* 61·8 m.p.h. (98·7 km./hr.). *Airframe:* ash, spruce and steel tube. *Propeller:* mahogany. *Covering:* aluminium (engine panels), plywood (fuselage) and unbleached linen (wings and tail).

## ALBATROS BIPLANE (Germany)

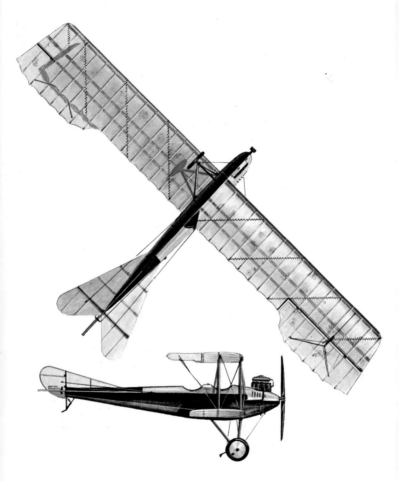

**64**

Typical Albatros 2-seat biplane of 1913–14. *Engine:* One 75 h.p. Mercedes 4-cylinder water-cooled in-line. *Span:* 47 ft. 6⅞ in. (14·50 m.). *Length:* 26 ft. 3 in. (8·00 m.). *Height:* approx. 10 ft. 9 in. (3·28 m.). *Wing area:* 480 sq. ft. (44·60 sq. m.). *Take-off weight:* approx. 2,756 lb. (1,250 kg.). *Speed:* 65 m.p.h. (105 km./hr.). *Airframe:* steel tube. *Propeller:* mahogany. *Covering:* aluminium (cowling), plywood (cockpit decking) and unbleached cotton (wings, tail and rear of fuselage).

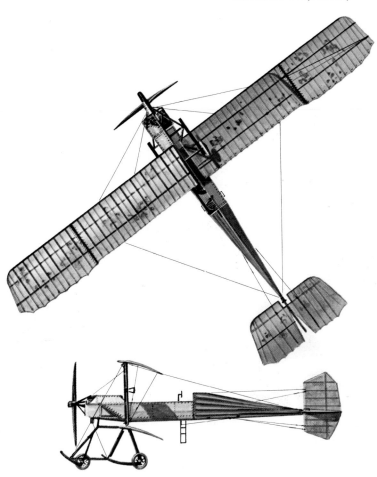

**65**

Breguet Type III (or U. 1), purchased for the Royal Swedish Army in 1912 and later designated B. 1. *Engine:* One 85 h.p. Salmson (Canton-Unné) 7-cylinder water-cooled radial. *Span:* 42 ft. 9⅔ in. (13·50 m.). *Length:* 27 ft. 0 in. (8·23 m.). *Height:* 9 ft. 10⅛ in. (3·00 m.). *Wing area:* 398·26 sq. ft. (37·00 sq. m.). *Empty weight:* 1,102 lb. (500 kg.). *Speed:* 62 m.p.h. (100 km./hr.). *Airframe:* steel tube and ash. *Propeller:* mahogany. *Covering:* aluminium (front of fuselage) and proofed linen and/or cotton (wings, tail and rear of fuselage).

## B.E.2a (U.K.)

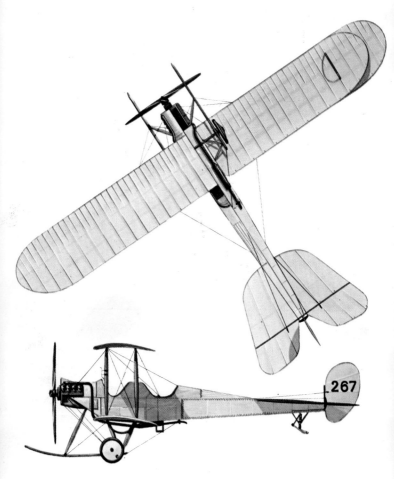

**66**

Royal Aircraft Factory-built B.E.2a of No. 2 Squadron R.F.C., 1913. *Engine:* One 70 h.p. Renault 8-cylinder air-cooled Vee-type. *Span:* 35 ft. 0½ in. (10·68 m.). *Length:* 29 ft. 6½ in. (9·00 m.). *Height:* 10 ft. 2 in. (3·10 m.). *Wing area:* 352 sq. ft. (32·70 sq. m.). *Take-off weight:* 1,600 lb. (726 kg.). *Speed:* 70 m.p.h. (113 km./hr.). *Airframe:* ash and spruce. *Propeller:* mahogany. *Covering:* aluminium and plywood (front of fuselage); unbleached linen (wings, tail and rear of fuselage).

**67**

Avro 504 prototype (modified), *ca.* November 1913. *Engine:* One 80 h.p. Gnome 7-cylinder rotary. *Span:* 36 ft. 0 in. (10·97 m.). *Length:* 29 ft. 3 in. (8·91 m.). *Height:* 10 ft. 4 in. (3·15 m.). *Wing area:* 342 sq. ft. (31·77 sq. m.). *Take-off weight:* 1,550 lb. (703 kg.). *Maximum speed:* 81 m.p.h. (130 km./hr.). *Airframe:* ash and spruce. *Propeller:* mahogany. *Covering:* aluminium (engine panels), plywood (cockpit decking), canvas (front of fuselage) and unbleached linen (wings, tail and rear of fuselage).

**B.S.1 (U.K.)**

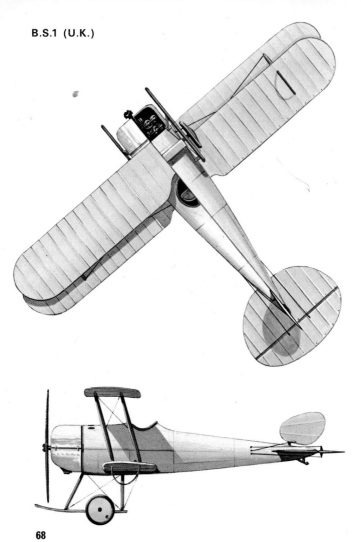

**68**

Royal Aircraft Factory B.S.1, early 1913. *Engine:* One 100 h.p. Gnome 10-cylinder two-row rotary. *Span:* 27 ft. 6 in. (8·38 m.). *Length:* 20 ft. 5¼ in. (6·23 m.). *Height:* 8 ft. 10 in. (2·69 m.). *Take-off weight:* 1,232 lb. (559 kg.). *Speed:* 92 m.p.h. (148 km./hr.). *Airframe:* ash and spruce. *Propeller:* mahogany. *Covering:* aluminium (cowling), birch ply (fuselage) and unbleached linen (wings and tail).

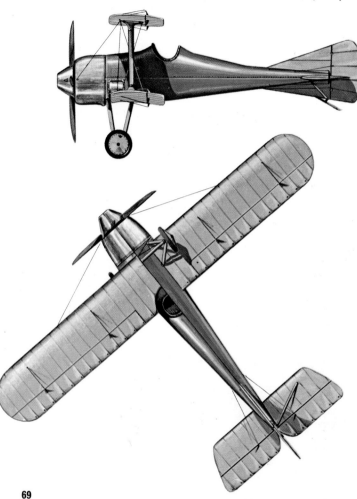

**69**

Royal Aircraft Factory S.E.4, *ca.* July 1914. *Engine:* One 160 h.p. Gnome 14-cylinder two-row rotary. *Span:* 27 ft. 6 in. (8·38 m.). *Length:* 21 ft. 0 in. (6·40 m.). *Height:* 9 ft. 10½ in. (3·01 m.). *Wing area:* 188 sq. ft. (17·47 sq. m.). *Speed:* 135 m.p.h. (217 km./hr.). *Airframe:* spruce, ash and steel tube. *Propeller:* mahogany. *Covering:* aluminium (cowling and spinner), plywood (fuselage) and unbleached linen (wings and tail).

## TABLOID (U.K.)

**70**

Sopwith Type S.S. (Tabloid) prototype, late 1913. *Engine:* One 80 h.p. Gnome 7-cylinder rotary. *Span:* 25 ft. 6 in. (7·77 m.). *Length:* 20 ft. 0 in. (6·10 m.). *Height:* 8 ft. 5 in. (2·57 m.). *Wing area:* 240 sq. ft. (22·30 sq. m.). *Take-off weight:* 1,060 lb. (481 kg.). *Speed:* 92 m.p.h. (148 km./hr.). *Airframe:* spruce and pine. *Propeller:* mahogany. *Covering:* aluminium (cowling and cockpit decking) and doped lightweight linen (wings, tail and rear of fuselage).

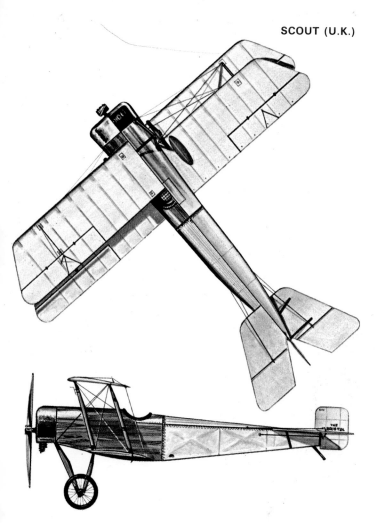

**71**

Bristol Scout prototype (later called Scout A), *ca.* March 1914. *Engine:* One 80 h.p. Gnome 7-cylinder rotary. *Span:* 22 ft. 0 in. (6·71 m.). *Length:* 19 ft. 9 in. (6·02 m.). *Height:* 8 ft. 6 in. (2·59 m.). *Wing area:* 161 sq. ft. (14·96 sq. m.). *Take-off weight:* 957 lb. (434 kg.). *Speed:* 95 m.p.h. (153 km./hr.). *Airframe:* ash, spruce and steel tube. *Propeller:* mahogany. *Covering:* Aluminium sheet (front of fuselage) and lightweight linen (wings, tail and rear of fuselage).

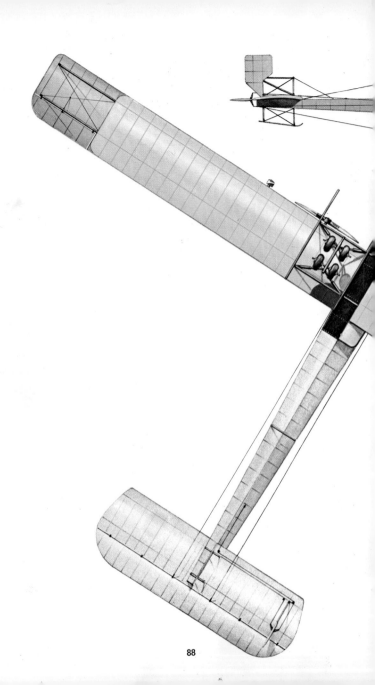

LE GRAND (Russia)

**72**

Sikorsky *Russkii Knyaz (Le Grand)*, spring 1913. *Engines:* Four 100 h.p. Argus 4-cylinder water-cooled in-lines. *Span:* 91 ft. 10⅓ in. (28·00 m.). *Length:* 62 ft. 4 in. (19·00 m.). *Height:* approx. 13 ft. 1½ in. (4·00 m.). *Take-off weight:* approx. 9,039 lb. (4,100 kg.). *Speed:* approx. 59 m.p.h. (95 km./hr.) at 3,280 ft. (1,000 m.). *Airframe:* spruce, pine and ash. *Propellers:* mahogany. *Covering:* mahogany plywood (front of fuselage) and rubber-proofed linen (wings, tail and rear of fuselage).

# SHORT FOLDER (U.K.)

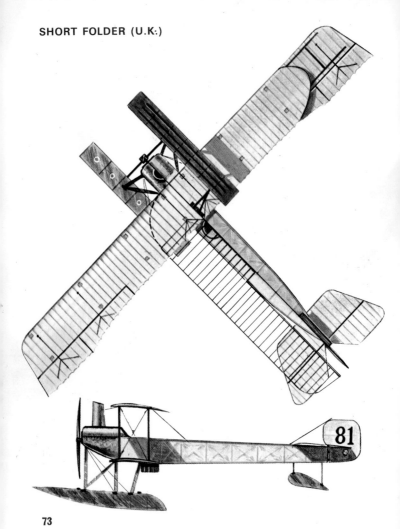

**73**

Short Folder S.64 for the R.N.A.S., at Eastchurch March 1914. *Engine:* One 160 h.p. Gnome 14-cylinder two-row rotary. *Span:* 56 ft. 0 in. (17·07 m.). *Width folded:* 12 ft. 0 in. (3·66 m.). *Length:* 40 ft. 0 in. (12·19 m.). *Height:* approx 12 ft. 0 in. (3·66 m.). *Wing area:* 550 sq. ft. (51·10 sq. m.). *Take-off weight:* 3,100 lb. (1,406 kg.). *Speed:* 78 m.p.h. (126 km./hr.). *Airframe:* steel tube, ash and spruce; sheet steel exhaust chimney. *Propeller:* mahogany. *Covering:* aluminium (cowling), plywood with ash rubbing strakes (floats) and unbleached cotton (fuselage, wings and tail).

# COANDA TURBINE AEROPLANE (Rumania/France)

**74**

Coanda turbine sesquiplane exhibited at the 2nd *Salon de l'Aéronautique,* Paris, October 1910. *Engine:* One 50 h.p. Clerget 4-cylinder water-cooled in-line. *Span:* 33 ft. 1⅝ in. (10·10 m.). *Length:* 39 ft. 7¼ in. (12·70 m.). *Height:* approx. 9 ft. 0¼ in. (2·75 m.). *Wing area:* 344·45 sq. ft. (32·00 sq. m.). *Take-off weight:* 926 lb. (420 kg.). *Airframe:* nickel-steel tube. *Covering:* varnished mahogany plywood.

## ELLEHAMMER II (Denmark)

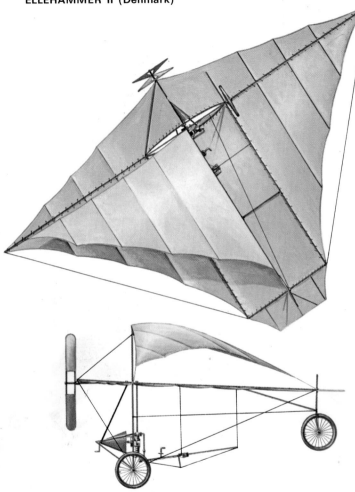

**75**

Ellehammer II 'semi-biplane', as flown at Lindholm, 12 September 1906. *Engine:* One 20 h.p. Ellehammer 3-cylinder air-cooled radial. *Span:* 30 ft. 11¾ in. (9·35 m.). *Length:* 20 ft. 4⅛ in. (6·20 m.). *Height:* 10 ft. 8⅜ in. (3·26 m.). *Wing area:* 398·26 sq. ft. (37·00 sq. m.). *Take-off weight:* approx. 397 lb. (180 kg.). *Speed:* 35 m.p.h. (57 km./hr.). *Airframe:* steel tube and mahogany. *Propeller:* tubular steel frame, canvas-covered blades. *Covering:* cotton canvas.

# ELLEHAMMER III (Denmark)

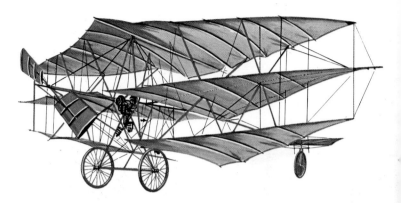

**76**

Ellehammer III triplane, 1907. *Engine:* One 30/35 h.p. Ellehammer 5-cylinder air-cooled radial. *Airframe:* steel tube and mahogany. *Propeller:* steel tube shafts, aluminium blades. *Covering:* cotton canvas. No other details known.

# ROE II (U.K.)

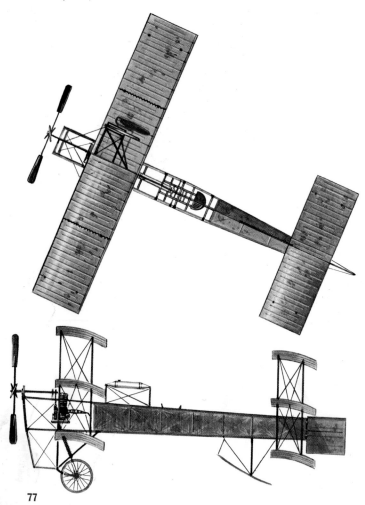

**77**

Roe II triplane as flown at Wembley Park, mid-December 1909. *Engine:* One 20 h.p. J.A.P. 4-cylinder water-cooled Vee-type. *Span:* 20 ft. 0 in. (6·10 m.). *Length:* 23 ft. 0 in. (7·01 m.). *Height:* 11 ft. 0 in. (3·35 m.). *Wing area:* 217·5 sq. ft. (20·21 sq. m.). *Take-off weight:* 400 lb. (181 kg.). *Speed:* 20 m.p.h. (32 km./hr.). *Airframe:* pine, ash, spruce and steel tube. *Propeller:* steel shafts, aluminium blades. *Covering:* Pegamoid proofed cotton.

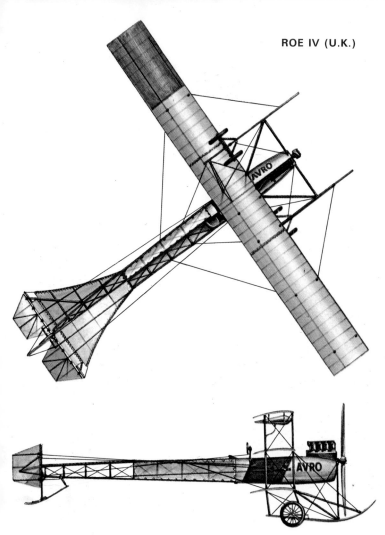

**ROE IV (U.K.)**

**78**

Roe IV triplane, *ca.* January 1911. *Engine:* One 35 h.p. Green 4-cylinder water-cooled in-line. *Span:* 32 ft. 0 in. (9·75 m.). *Length:* 30 ft. 0 in. (9·14 m.). *Height:* 9 ft. 0 in. (2·74 m.). *Wing area:* 294 sq. ft. (27·31 sq. m.). *Take-off weight:* 650 lb. (295 kg.). *Airframe:* ash, poplar and steel tube. *Propeller:* mahogany. *Covering:* aluminium (front of fuselage) and unbleached cotton (centre of fuselage, wings and tail).

# PHILLIPS 'MULTIPLANE' (U.K.)

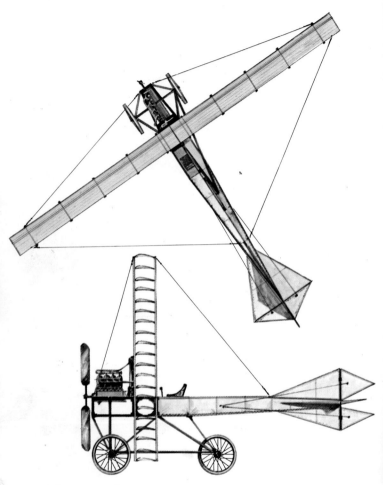

**79**

Horatio Phillips 'multiplane' No. 1, *ca.* 1904. *Engine:* One 22 h.p. Phillips 4-cylinder water-cooled in-line. *Span:* 17 ft. 9 in. (5·41 m.). *Length:* 13 ft. 9 in. (4·19 m.). *Height:* 10 ft. 0 in. (3·05 m.). *Take-off weight:* 600 lb. (272 kg.). *Speed:* 34 m.p.h. (55 km./hr.). *(All data estimated.) Airframe:* spruce, ash and steel tube (fuselage); aerofoil sustainers of yellow pine. *Propeller:* steel shafts, aluminium blades. *Covering (fuselage and tail):* unbleached calico.

**Albatros** 64

In its early years, the Albatros-Werke G.m.b.H. of Johannisthal bei Berlin acquired its initial experience in the realm of aviation by building foreign designs under licence. It chose these well, for the two most important types undertaken were the excellent Antoinette and Etrich *Taube* monoplanes. The *Taube* in particular exercised a strong influence upon Albatros' own early designs, although the latter were mostly biplane types.

At the Berlin Air Exhibitions of 1912 and 1913 the Albatros company displayed two enclosed-cabin *Taube*-type monoplanes, and a biplane whose wing and tail contours were also strikingly similar to those of the Austrian design. A feature of early Albatros biplanes was the unusual configuration of the radiator, installed under the nose and shaped to follow the curved contour of the lower engine cowling. One such machine, exhibited at Berlin in 1913, had a four-wheel, twin-skid main landing gear and mounted a searchlight between the mainplanes on the starboard side for use when making night flights. Another version, powered by a fully-cowled Daimler engine with a frontal radiator, had raised decking round the two cockpits, non-over-hanging ailerons, the lower wings set below the fuselage and a wheels-only main undercarriage instead of the more usual wheels and centre skid arrangement of early Albatroses.

These various designs were the forerunners of the unarmed military B types and the subsequent wartime C types built by Albatros, and were themselves responsible for several impressive pre-war performances. Josef Sablatnig, a well-known competition flier in Germany and later the constructor of a series of successful wartime seaplanes, piloted an Albatros carrying three passengers to an altitude of 9,282 ft. (2,830 m.) at Johannisthal on 28 September 1913. Like the *Taube* – which, flown solo, could remain in the air for more than five hours – the Albatroses were also noted for their powers of endurance. On 27–28 June 1914 one of the military biplanes, flown by Landmann, stayed aloft over Johannisthal for a record 21 hr. 50 min., during which he covered more than 1,200 miles (1,931 km.) through the air. His record was short-lived, for on 10–11 July Reinhold Böhm, in the same machine and carrying a 132 Imp. gal. (600 litre) fuel load, remained airborne for 24 hr. 12 min. to complete the first 24-hour nonstop flight over a closed circuit in aviation history.

**Antoinette** 42 & 58

The Société Antoinette was named after the daughter of Jules Gastambide, the company's director, but its leading figure was Léon Levavasseur, the engineer and former artist responsible for its major products during the first decade of powered flight in Europe. Indeed, had it not been for the excellent range of Antoinette engines – produced originally to power motor-boats – available from 1903, there seems little doubt that aviation in

Europe would have progressed even more slowly than it did. Levavasseur's first full-size aeroplane, a bird-like monoplane tested in 1903, was an utter failure, and it was not until summer 1907 that he completed (in model form) his next design. Of curious appearance, it was a monoplane with a cruciform tail and a pusher propeller at the back driven by a shaft from the engine, which was mounted midway along the fuselage. A full-size machine, identified as the Antoinette I, was brought almost to completion in 1908 and then abandoned. The Antoinette II was the designation of the rebuilt Gastambide-Mengin I which crashed after making four hop-flights at Bagatelle in February 1908. Reflown at Issy on 22 July 1908, it gave a foretaste of the future classic Antoinette monoplanes, and on 21 August made the first circular flight by a monoplane during a flight lasting just over 1½ min. Antoinette III was the alternative title of the Ferber IX, a tractor biplane designed by Capitaine F. Ferber which was abandoned after only a few trial flights in August and September 1908.

The first of the classic Antoinette monoplanes was the Antoinette IV, flown for the first time at Issy on 9 October 1908. Levavasseur's artistic sense was apparent in every one of its elegant lines, from the slender boat-shaped fuselage to the delicately arched wings and bird-like tail assembly. The Antoinette IV was powered by a 50 h.p. Antoinette engine, weighed 1,014 lb. (460 kg.), and in its original form had wings with a total area of 322·9 sq. ft. (30 sq. m.). These were rigged with dihedral – a feature long known but little used before the appearance of the Antoinette – and their undersides had a shallower curve than the top surfaces, giving a thick aerofoil cross-section. Trapezoidal ailerons were attached to the outer trailing edges to provide lateral control. The longest flight recorded for the Antoinette IV in this form was 2,953 ft. (900 m.) on 18 November 1908; but during the following winter the wing area was increased substantially, to 538·2 sq. ft. (50 sq. m.), and on 19 February 1909 a 3 mile (5 km.) flight was made at Mourmelon. From the latter part of March the aeroplane was flown almost exclusively by Hubert Latham, in whose hands its performance improved rapidly. On 19 July 1909, Latham left Sangatte, near Calais, in an attempt to fly the English Channel in the Antoinette IV. Unfortunately, engine failure brought him down in the water some 7½ miles (12 km.) from the French coast, but the buoyancy of the aircraft's deep wings stood him in good stead until he could be picked up by the destroyer *Harpon*. The Antoinette IV figured prominently at the Rheims meeting a little later in the year, where it earned for Latham the second prize in the *Grand Prix* and on 26 August 1909 set up its own best flight of 96·06 miles (154·6 km.), lasting 2 hr. 17 min. 21·4 sec.

The Antoinette V, which had meanwhile made its first flight on

20 December 1908, differed some-what in having triangular ailerons, and increased vertical tail area including a small rectangular rudder sandwiched between two triangular fins. Its performance, however, was inferior to the Antoinette IV, and this may have influenced Leva-vasseur in taking the retrograde step, in the Antoinette VI and all subsequent machines, of discarding aileron-type controls altogether in favour of wing-warping. Little is recorded of the Antoinette VI, which made its maiden flight on 17 April 1909, but in any event the Antoinette VII, despite an in-auspicious start to its career, was a much superior aeroplane. It was built specifically for Hubert Latham, who hoped to use it in a renewed bid to fly the Channel, but again he was unsuccessful. The distinction of making the first cross-Channel flight went to Louis Blériot on 25 July 1909, but two days later Latham took up the Antoinette VII – on its maiden flight – to try and beat Blériot's time. Again he was unlucky, the machine ditching this time when he was only a mile offshore. However, the Antoinette VII was salvaged and rebuilt and, like Latham's other machine, vindi-cated itself at Rheims by flying to a height of 508·53 ft. (155 m.) to take the *Prix de l'Altitude*. Also at Rheims was the Antoinette VIII, which first flew on 15 August 1909, but this machine failed to win any prizes. The Antoinette VII was the undoubted success of the year, and formed the basis of standard pro-duction machines built subse-quently; one at least had a 50 h.p. Gnome engine, and the Albatros-Werke G.m.b.H. of Johannisthal built the Antoinette under licence during 1910.

The other Antoinette design chosen for illustration was also associated with Latham, being pro-duced to his specification as a competitor in the 1911 *Concours Militaire*, also held at Rheims. A three-seat monoplane, it was a failure from the flying point of view, but in terms of design technique was years ahead of its time. In an effort to achieve maximum per-formance no trouble was spared to eliminate every possible external excrescence. The wings were fully cantilevered, with even the warp control wires buried inside them; the main landing wheels were en-cased in wide 'trouser' fairings, earning the machine the nickname *Jupe-Culotte*; and the three-man crew entered the fully-streamlined fuselage through a door in the underside, their seats being covered overhead by a transparent fairing. But the *Type Latham*, also known as the 'Monobloc', for all its ingenious design, was hastily built and, with its original 50 h.p. engine, under-powered, and it only left the ground for a few yards. A description in *The Aeroplane* of 21 September 1911 quotes a 100 h.p. engine, an overall length of 37 ft. 8¾ in. (11·50 m.) and ten landing wheels (two main sets of four and two tail wheels); illustrations in *l'Aérophile* of 15 January 1912 give a length of 40 ft. 2¼ in. (12·25 m.) and reveal two main sets of three wheels with a single skid beneath the tail. However, these various modifications evidently brought no effective increase in performance, and the aeroplane was eventually abandoned, but it is noteworthy for the influence that it undoubtedly had on future designs.

**Barber** 2

Partly due to the brevity of his aeronautical career, Horatio Barber (born 1875) usually receives scant attention from historians, but his Valkyrie canard monoplanes were safe, reliable machines, if a little unorthodox. In a period when many pilots, skilful or otherwise, often came to grief when landing on uneven ground, the Valkyrie's wide-set skids rendered it much less liable to overturn, as well as facilitating the forward bracing of the wings.

In June 1909 Barber formed the Aeronautical Syndicate Ltd., to build and test the Valkyrie monoplanes, and the first were tried out on Salisbury Plain during late 1909 and 1910. When the new Hendon Aerodrome was opened by Louis Blériot on 1 October 1910, A.S.L. transferred its activities there, renting three of the eight available sheds and advertising tuition and daily passenger flights.

Three basic Valkyrie types were built. The original No. 1 machine was of Type A, the standard single-seat version shown in the illustration. The second version to appear was the Type C, a larger aircraft with a 39 ft. 0 in. (11·89 m.) wing span, capable of carrying a pilot and two passengers; while the Type B of 1911 was a single-seat cross-country racer. The Type B had twin one-piece rudders carried further aft on boom extensions (as did the Valkyrie C), the length thus being increased to 26 ft. 0 in. (7·92 m.). The wing span was shortened to 31 ft. 0 in. (9·45 m.), the fixed foreplane reduced slightly in size, and the gap between the port and starboard skids widened by an extra 1 ft. 0 in. (0·30 m.). Powerplant was a 50 h.p. Gnome.

Barber's faith in the dependability of his aircraft is expressed in a comment from R. Dallas Brett's *History of British Aviation*: 'Mr. Barber . . . demonstrated the quick take-off of his mount by repeatedly charging at the crowd from a distance of fifty yards and pulling the machine off over their heads.' Altogether some twenty Valkyries were built up to April 1912, and so far as is known they were involved in only two fatalities. In the first of these the aircraft and its engine were completely exonerated, and the second was clearly caused by a cocksure pilot trying to show off before he had properly familiarised himself with the machine. At a meeting held at Hendon in 1911 for visiting politicians to assess the military promise of various aircraft Barber was refused permission to demonstrate the Valkyrie. However, this did not prevent him, a little later, from offering four of these aircraft to the government for evaluation by the War Office and Admiralty. The second casualty mentioned above was the Army lieutenant who had arrived at Hendon on 17 September to collect the first of these machines. After the accident it seems likely that the aircraft were never claimed; at any rate they do not appear in the initial listings when military serial numbers were first allocated in the following summer.

Nevertheless, in 1911 Barber carried 151 passengers in his Valkyries without incident, and altogether flew more than 7,000 miles (11,265 km.) during the year. On 4 July 1911 he created a little piece of history by flying from Shoreham to Hove with the first item of freight ever sent by air: a carton of Osram electric light bulbs. He donated the £100 that he received to the Royal Aero Club, which used the money to endow the Britannia Trophy, awarded annually from 1913 to 'the British aviator(s) accomplishing the most meritorious performance in the air during the preceding year'. Barber's other ventures were rather less successful. A tractor biplane called the Viking appeared early in 1912, having between-wing ailerons and a 50 h.p. Gnome driving two outboard propellers. It apparently flew reasonably well, but was not a practical design, despite modification later to a single-tractor layout and a twin-float landing gear. Barber was also the inspiration behind J. D. North's curious 1913 design for the Grahame-White company to compete with the Vickers E.F.B.1 and the Royal Aircraft Factory's gun-carrying biplanes. Of this, Dallas Brett drily commented that Barber

'ought to have known better'. In April 1912 Barber found rising development costs too much for him and closed down the company, the stock being purchased by Handley Page.

## Blackburn 37 & 47

Robert Blackburn, born in 1885 into a family with an engineering background, himself became a qualified civil engineer and was working in Rouen at the time of Wilbur Wright's visit to France in 1908. He became an immediate convert to the cause of aviation. The design of his first aeroplane was begun in Paris, but Blackburn soon returned to Britain, where the aeroplane was assembled in a Leeds workshop. As was to be expected, it was soundly and solidly constructed, for which reason it is customarily referred to as the 'Blackburn heavy monoplane'. Authorities disagree whether or not the design was influenced by Santos-Dumont's *Demoiselle*, though their overall similarities seem too numerous to be attributed to mere coincidence. The major difference lay in the installation of the Blackburn type's engine beneath the wings, supported by the main chassis frame and having an overhead chain-belt drive to the propeller; this was not Santos's normal practice, though such an installation was made in November 1908 on his No. 19bis, which never flew. Both types had a cruciform tail assembly, performing the dual functions of rudder and elevator, and Blackburn also utilised a sliding seat to control the fore and aft balance. The Blackburn 'heavy' was originally projected with a 24 ft. 0 in. (7·32 m.) wing span, but a larger wing was fitted when the machine began its trials on the sands at Marske in north-eastern Yorkshire in the spring of 1909. After some preliminary taxying tests, Blackburn made a successful take-off, but when he tried to execute a turn the aircraft went into a side-slip and crashed. It was not rebuilt.

There can be no doubt about the inspiration behind Blackburn's second monoplane, which was a much more attractive venture clearly based on the French Antoinette. Using a 38 ft. 4 in. (11·68 m.) wing of basically similar construction and camber to that of the first aeroplane, Blackburn installed an Isaacson radial engine borrowed from its inventor; this was currently developing about 40 h.p., although intended ultimately to give an output of 60 h.p. The monoplane was taken to Blackpool in August 1910 with the object of entering it for various events, but it was not ready in time. Early in 1911 it was flown, but on an early flight it crashed and the Isaacson engine was destroyed. The aircraft was rebuilt and recommenced trials with a 50 h.p. Gnome, later appearing at the Olympia Aero Show in March 1911. By this time Blackburn had made a valuable addition to his staff in the person of B. C. Hucks, who took over the test flying of the aircraft and was chiefly responsible for its subsequent improvement. During 1912–14, Hucks was generally considered among the best half dozen pilots in Britain, and few had his all-round experience of flying.

Variants of the second Blackburn monoplane were produced in 1910–11 with the name Mercury; they were 2-seaters and most were powered by 50 h.p. Gnome or 60 h.p. Green engines. Probably about a dozen were built, several being used to equip the flying school which Blackburn set up at Filey in 1911. Two Gnome-engined Mercurys were entered for the £10,000 *Daily Mail* Circuit of Britain race in 1911, but one was a non-starter and the other (flown by Hucks) was obliged to withdraw later because of engine trouble. Preliminary tests were started in November 1911 of another Mercury variant with a 60 h.p. Renault engine; but on 6 December its pilot, Hubert Oxley, failed to pull out soon enough from a dive, and both he and his passenger were killed in the resulting crash. However, despite these and other lesser mishaps the basic Mercury design continued to develop, if not exactly to flourish, and by 1913 bore little resemblance to the original archetype. Typical of the later machines is the single-seater owned by the Shuttleworth Trust, which is the oldest British aeroplane still in flying condition. Two similar, but 2-seat, variants of this were built in 1913, one for Doctor M. G. Christie and the other for display at the 1914 Aero Show at Olympia. The latter machine had a communal cockpit with no separate decking round the two seats.

Two Type E monoplanes were

built in 1912 for the Military Trials, although neither competed in the event. These, too, were based on the Mercury, one being powered by a 60 h.p. Green engine and the other by a 60 h.p. Renault. Greater use was made of steel tube in the airframe, and a distinctively curved decking was fitted around and to the rear of the cockpits. In May 1913 Blackburn was invited to participate in production of the Royal Aircraft Factory's B.E.2c, with an initial contract for a dozen machines. This may have had some influence on the Type L, which was also a tractor biplane, the first of its type to be designed by Blackburn. Work on the Type L, a 2-seat, twin-float seaplane with a 130 h.p. Salmson engine, was begun in 1913 with a view to entering the aircraft in the 1914 Circuit of Britain race. The outbreak of war prevented the race from being held, but the Type L was later purchased by the Admiralty, so beginning a long and fruitful career by Blackburn of building aeroplanes for the Royal Navy.

## Bland 19

A grand-daughter of the Dean of Belfast, Lilian Bland was a sports writer and photographer in London in the early years of the 20th century when her imagination was caught by the cross-Channel flight of Louis Blériot in the summer of 1909. Determined to prove that flying was not the exclusive prerogative of the male sex, she immediately began to acquaint herself with the principles of flight and the work of the leading pioneers before returning to Northern Ireland for the purpose of building an aeroplane of her own. Taking a leaf out of the Wrights' book, she decided to build first a glider, which if successful could be fitted with a motor at a later date. Christened 'Mayfly', it was an equal-span biplane with twin forward elevators, a single rudder at the rear and a twin-skid landing gear. Several tethered tests were carried out at Carnmoney, Co. Antrim, followed by a number of short soaring hops from a towed start. Many of these were made with the assistance of a downhill slope for take-off, but the basic validity of the design proved itself to the point where Miss Bland, in a letter to *Flight* in February 1910, could claim that 'My only difficulty is at present to prevent her flying when I do not want her to'.

In June 1910 Lilian Bland came to England to collect the little 2-cylinder engine for the Mayfly that A. V. Roe had built to her order. When she reached home with it, the fuel tank had still not been delivered, but she was so impatient to test the new engine that she rigged an empty whiskey bottle in its place, feeding the fuel to the motor via her aunt's ear trumpet. She later recorded that 'as the engine is English its sense of humour is not developed sufficiently for these proceedings'. In its powered form the Mayfly had a 6 ft. 6 in. (1·98 m.) adjustable pitch Avro propeller; other modifications from the original glider included between-wing ailerons, twin elevators fore and aft (operated by a bicycle handlebar control), a small fixed central tailplane and single rudder, and wheels as well as skids for landing. It was transported to nearby Randalstown Park and reassembled for flight testing, the first hop-flights being made in August 1910.

The Mayfly was perhaps most remarkable as a manifestation of its originator's determination to succeed. It could not be called a practical design – in fact it was only 'designed' at all in the broadest sense of the word, for it was assembled without benefit of engineering knowledge on the part of Miss Bland and her helpers; no great effort was expended to rig it square or true, and it sagged and bulged in all directions. Nevertheless it flew, and Lilian Bland taught herself to fly on it. She realised, however, that it was underpowered, while at the same time a bigger engine would have shaken it to pieces. This, and the prohibitive cost of developing it further, persuaded her to yield to her father's plea to give up her flying experiments, and she emigrated to Canada in 1912, returning to England in 1935. The Mayfly's Avro engine is believed to be the one now in the possession of the Science Museum in London.

**Blériot**  35 & 46
Louis Blériot, born at Cambrai, France, in 1872, ranks with Henry Farman and Léon Levavasseur among the truly dominant figures during the early years of powered flight in Europe. From an established business in the motor car accessory industry he was attracted to aviation at the turn of the century, building an experimental model ornithopter (the Blériot I) in 1901–2. His first full-size aeroplane, the Blériot II, was a float-mounted glider biplane built for him by the Voisin brothers and closely resembled the contemporary Voisin-Archdeacon glider seaplane. On 18 July 1905 it rose from the Seine at Billancourt, but almost immediately fell back into the water, nearly drowning Gabriel Voisin in the process, and no further attempts were made to fly it. The Blériot III was also a floatplane, with annular lifting surfaces fore and aft each forming a continuous ellipse. Such an arrangement was eye-catching but impractical, and when tested on the Lac d'Enghien in May 1906 it failed to leave the water. It was (apart from Levavasseur's own 1903 aeroplane) the first European aircraft to utilise the splendid little 24 h.p. Antoinette V-8 engine, which drove two small tractor propellers. Later in 1906 Blériot converted this machine into the Blériot IV, installing two Antoinettes driving pusher propellers, retaining the annular tail surface, but replacing the forward one by orthodox biplane wings (with small, narrow ailerons) and adding a frontal elevator. Taken on to the lake in October 1906 it still refused to fly; nor, at Bagatelle a month later (now as a landplane with one 50 h.p. Antoinette), did it show any more promise and Blériot abandoned it.

He now diverted his attention –

with what success later events were to show – to the development of a practical monoplane. Completed not long after the flights of Santos-Dumont's 14*bis*, the Blériot V also followed a canard layout. It was a curious machine, with oddly curved and cambered wings covered with varnished paper and mounting a 24 h.p. Antoinette engine at the rear. It made a few short hops at Bagatelle in April 1907 but was wrecked after the fourth attempt. The influence of Trajan Vuia (*q.v.*) became evident in the Blériot VI, his first tractor-type monoplane. Based on a Langley design and constructed for him by Louis Peyret, it had tandem-mounted, cantilever wings with a considerable dihedral angle, and pivoting tips to the front pair, which acted as elevators. Vertical surfaces comprised a long, shallow fin and a small rudder. Nicknamed *Libellule* (Dragonfly), the Blériot VI made nearly a dozen hop-flights at Issy in July and August 1907, the longest being 492 ft. (150 m.). Later, with a 50 h.p. engine (thought to have been a 16-cylinder), a smaller fin and reduced dihedral, it made another six flights, the best covering 604 ft. (184 m.) on 17 September.

The Blériot VII, which appeared at the end of 1907, marked a significant advance in performance, and an even greater one in terms of design. Remarkably sophisticated for its time, it had a completely covered fuselage, low-mounted cantilever wings and a fully-enclosed Antoinette driving a 4-blade metal propeller. There were elevons and a rudder, but no fixed tail surfaces. Some half a dozen flights were made at Issy in November and December 1907, two being over 1,640 ft. (500 m.), and speeds up to 50 m.p.h. (80 km/hr.) were attained. On 18 December, the aircraft was totally wrecked on landing. The monoplane line continued with the Blériot VIII, flown for the first time on 17 June 1908 and notable for the small triangular ailerons at its wingtips. It had an open-framework fuselage, a square rudder and a fixed tailplane with pivoting-elevator tips. In July it was modified into the VIII*bis* by having the first flap-type ailerons ever fitted to an aeroplane; and it became the VIII*ter* in September when these were replaced by pivoting wingtip elevons and a fixed, separate tailplane was added. From the flight of 2,297 ft. (700 m.) that was the original Blériot VIII's best performance, these successive modifications led to a three-stage round-trip flight of 17·4 miles (28 km.) by the Blériot VIII*ter* on 31 October 1908. In its various guises the Blériot VIII made more than 30 flights.

Three Blériot machines were on show at the *Salon de l'Automobile et de l'Aéronautique* in December 1908. Of these the Blériot IX was another tractor monoplane with a 100 h.p. Antoinette, and the Blériot X, curiously, a pusher biplane; but the former made only a few very brief hops and the latter was never completed. The third machine, however, was the one destined to make Blériot's reputation and fortune and to establish, with the Antoinette designs, the classic tractor monoplane formula of the pre-war years. It is now considered that Raymond Saulnier played a large part in the actual design of the Blériot XI. As originally displayed, and as flown for the first time at Issy on 23 January 1909, it had a 30 h.p. R.E.P. engine with a crude 4-blade metal propeller, and a small kite-shaped fin was fixed above the wing-warping pylons. The fin was removed after the Blériot XI was taken in for alteration early in April, and the R.E.P. was replaced by a 25 h.p. Anzani engine with a Chauvière propeller. After the early experiments with ailerons, whose purpose Blériot did not properly understand, the Blériot XI relied entirely on wing-warping for its lateral control, and was the first European aircraft to employ this system really effectively. During the spring and summer the Type XI continued to make many excellent flights, including one early in July lasting over 50 minutes.

In October 1908 Lord Northcliffe, proprietor of the London *Daily Mail*, had offered a prize of £1,000 to the first aviator to fly across the English Channel from coast to coast in either direction; and in the early hours of 25 July 1909 Blériot took off in the Type XI from Les Baraques, near Calais, landing in a field near Dover Castle little more than half an hour later. His attempt, made only on impulse after the accident to Latham's Antoinette (*q.v.*), was not accomplished without a certain element of luck, and Blériot's landing at Dover damaged the

undercarriage and propeller. But nothing could detract from his success, the political and military repercussions from which were enormous. It also captured the imagination of the general public: in London 120,000 people went to see the aeroplane during the four days that it was displayed in Selfridge's Oxford Street store. His welcome on returning to Paris was even more enthusiastic, and the Blériot XI was soon in production, at first for competitive fliers such as Leblanc and Delagrange and later in substantial quantities for the *Aviation Militaire*. Developed versions of the Type XI were in widespread use, in England as well as in France, during the early part of World War I and are described in the *Bombers 1914–19* volume of this series. The Channel flight aircraft is now in the custody of the *Conservatoire des Arts et Métiers* in Paris. Before the Channel flight Blériot himself had set greater store by his Type XII, a larger monoplane with a high wing layout that was flown for the first time on 21 May 1909. This had a pendulum-type chassis arrangement basically similar to the Santos-Dumont *Demoiselle* and the Blackburn 'heavy' monoplane, with engine and pilot at floor level to give a low centre of gravity and greater stability. The original engine, a 35 h.p. E.N.V., was later exchanged for a 60 h.p. unit of the same make. The wings were rigid, but two small ailerons were mounted low down on the chassis abreast of the pilot. The Type XII's chief drawback was its poor directional control, which led to a variety of successive tail configurations, but otherwise it performed well. Blériot's aim had been to produce an aeroplane capable of lifting more than just its pilot, and this was realised on 12 June 1909 when it became the first aircraft to fly with two passengers. It made an excellent endurance flight of 29·35 miles (47·23 km.) at Douai on 3 July, but crashed and burnt out while being flown by Blériot at the Rheims meeting in the following month. One Blériot XII, named *White Eagle*, was the first aircraft owned by Claude Grahame-White (*q.v.*). The Blériot XIII, also a competitor at Rheims, was generally similar except in having a 50 h.p. Anzani engine.

Subsequent Blériot types during the period under review included the 'Big Bat' of 1910; the *Aérobus* of 1911, which made a 3 mile (5 km.) flight on 23 March with 11 passengers; and the Type XXVII, produced for the 1911 Gordon Bennett race and powered by a 50 h.p. Gnome engine. On 23 September 1910 the young Peruvian pilot George Chavez made the first aircraft flight over the Alps in a Blériot monoplane, and on 23 October 1911 Captain Piazza of the Italian Army air service carried out the first flight ever made by an aeroplane in an active warlike capacity – a one-hour reconnaissance flight from Tripoli to Aziza in a Blériot XI*bis*. One of the leading exponents of the Blériot's qualities was the Frenchman Adolphe Pégoud, whose Type XI-2 (80 h.p. Gnome) is now in the hands of the *Musée de l'Air* in Paris. Pégoud's aerobatic feats in France and Great Britain made him a star attraction wherever he went. He was the first man to parachute from an aeroplane (19 August 1913) and was also one of the earliest to perform the manoeuvre of looping (21 September 1913).

## Borel 3

After an early association with the Morane brothers, Gabriel Borel started a flying school north of Paris at Vidamée, and by the end of 1911 was established as an aeroplane manufacturer in his own right. A 2-seat monoplane of Borel design, with an 80 h.p. Gnome engine, was tested in France with some success, and it was probably an aircraft of this type that was entered for the British Military Trials of August 1912, but which failed to put in an appearance. Also during 1912, a seaplane version was tested at St. Malo. This had twin catamaran-type main floats and a steerable tail float, was some 27 ft. 0 in. (8·23 m.) in overall length and had a wing span of 37 ft. 6 in. (11·43 m.). It was less successful than the landplane, but marked the start of Borel's predilection for water-borne aircraft that continued up to and during World War 1.

The Borel seaplane exhibited at the Olympia Aero Show in February 1913 differed principally in having a bull-nosed cowling for its Gnome engine, and was evidently a more efficient machine. Seventeen similar aircraft had already been ordered by the Italian Navy, and eight more were to be completed for the Royal Naval Air Service, six of them by Delacombe and Maréchal. The first Borel for Britain was collected from Buc in May 1913 by Gordon Bell, whose return trip was a rather hazardous affair. He eventually made a safe landing after the machine was put into a side-slip – a manoeuvre which, as Dallas Brett later recorded, was then 'popularly regarded as being in the nature of a preliminary funeral rite'. A 'hot rod' version of the Borel seaplane, with a 160 h.p. Gnome engine, was entered by Georges Chemet for the 1913 seaplane races at Monaco, but was eliminated after an early taxying accident without showing its capabilities.

During the spring of 1913 a new Borel product, designed by Odier, also made its appearance. Radically different from the standard Borel configuration, this machine was a military monoplane with a pusher-engined layout and a wheel/skid land undercarriage. A trio of steel booms, forming a triangular section, supported the tail assembly, the uppermost boom passing through the propeller boss to act as a bearing for the 80 h.p. Gnome engine. The 2-man nacelle was about 10 ft. 0 in. (3·05 m.) in length, the seats being side by side with the observer's seat to the left and some 9¾ in. (25 cm.) ahead of the pilot's, to give the former a clear field of vision and fire. The undercarriage immediately below the cockpit was deliberately made free of cross-struts or bracing wires to enable bombs or other objects to be dropped overboard. At a slightly later stage than the illustration portrays, the nacelle was armoured all over with 3 mm. nickel-chrome steel plate, and a metal-framed windscreen placed in front of the occupants. At the end of the year the Borel stand at the Paris *Salon* included an even more freakish design, of similar concept to the earlier Tatin-Paulhan *Aéro-Torpille* in that it had its engine mounted amidships in a fully covered fuselage, with an extension shaft to a propeller mounted behind the tail. A machine-gun was mounted in the foremost of the two cockpits.

## Breguet 65

Descendants of a celebrated French family of clock and instrument makers, Louis (1880–1955) and Jacques (1881–1939) Breguet founded one of today's oldest aircraft manufacturing companies. Their initial powered flight ventures, in association with Professor Charles Richet, were the *gyroplanes* built and tested in 1906–8 and described in the *Helicopters* volume of this series. The Breguet brothers turned to fixed-wing machines in 1909, exhibiting an engine-less pusher biplane at Olympia in March. This aeroplane never flew, at least not in its original configuration, for the Breguet I* and all other Breguet products up to the Type X of 1914 followed a tractor layout. First flown at La Brayelle, near Douai, on 28 June 1909, the Breguet I was

* A retrospective designation: at first, following on from the three *gyroplanes*, it was called the Breguet IV.

noteworthy for its extensive use of metal construction. Steel tube was used for the airframe, including the wing spars and single interplane struts, and the ribs were of aluminium; the only substantial wooden items were the long parallel runners. The 39 ft. 4½ in. (12·00 m.) wings were each built in three sections, the short centre-sections being flanked by side-curtains to form a 'box' around the single-seat, coffin-shaped nacelle. The four outer sections could be warped differentially or in unison to act either as ailerons or as elevators. A biplane tail with twin rudders formed another 'box' at the rear. The 3-blade metal propeller was driven by a 50 h.p. Antoinette, but by the time of the Rheims meeting in August 1909 this had been exchanged for a Renault of similar power and the aeroplane had undergone various other improvements, justifying the new designation I*bis*. The side-curtains had been removed, the span of the upper tailplane increased, the skid runners shortened and balancing wheels added beneath the lower wingtips (previously they had been mounted outboard of the wings on a level with the front spar). The Breguet I*bis* was damaged while landing from its third flight at Rheims, and was presumably abandoned thereafter, for Breguet's next design was totally different in conception.

The new tractor biplane set the basic pattern followed by all subsequent Breguet designs up to 1914. Precise designations for these are difficult to establish, but the two major versions seem to have been the L.1 (sometimes called the 'cruiser') a 2-seater of 1911 with a 60 h.p. Renault motor, and the 2/3-seat Type III, to which a variety of engines were fitted. Breguet biplanes of this period were characterised by cruciform tail control surfaces, attached behind the fuselage by means of a universal pivot. Distinguishing features of the L.1 included a separate fixed tailplane, mounted under the fuselage ahead of the elevator; lower wings less than two-thirds the span of the upper ones; and a tricycle or quadricycle wheel-and-skid undercarriage. The forward component of this assembly was steerable, and sometimes mounted a small vertical vane on the front supporting strut. In September 1911 a Breguet L.1 flown by Bregi made a pioneering flight from Casablanca to Fez with a cargo of air mail letters. Known as the 'Breguet du Maroc', it is now in the possession of the *Conservatoire des Arts et Métiers* in Paris.

The Breguet Type III was the basis of the military models employed by France and Britain prior to the outbreak of World War 1. Following the *Concours Militaire* in 1911, six Breguets were ordered for the French Army. The usual power-plant at that time was the 50 or 80 h.p. Gnome, with which the type was designated G.3. Prefix letters L or U signified a Renault or Salmson (Canton-Unné) engine, and HU a seaplane (*Hydravion*) with a Salmson engine. A few U.3's were still in service with *Escadrille* Br.17 of the *Aviation Militaire* in August

1914. The U.3's in British service had either the 85 or 110 h.p. Salmson (Canton-Unné) radial. They had wings of nearly equal span, no fixed tailplane, circular-section fuselages and a wheels-only undercarriage. A very early British Breguet bore the legend 'B.3' on the rudder, the prefix letter indicating a tractor aircraft. Three Breguets appear in the initial listing of serial numbers for Admiralty aeroplanes, five others in the first batch of Army serials. Because of its metal construction and near-tubular shape, the Canton-Unné Breguet was quickly dubbed 'Tin Whistle' by British Naval pilots. The Type X, mentioned earlier, was more strongly built than its frail predecessors, and had a 160 h.p. Gnome. On an aircraft of this type Louis Breguet earned the Croix de Guerre for a valuable reconnaissance of enemy troop movements shortly before the Battle of the Marne in September 1914.

**Bristol** 13, 52, 53 & 71
The British and Colonial Aeroplane Co. was the operative one of four companies formed in February 1910 by Sir George White, Chairman of the Bristol Tramways and Carriage Co., and members of his family. A licence was obtained to build and market in Britain the Zodiac biplane, a variant of the Voisin boxkite biplane, and one of these machines was displayed on the Bristol stand at Olympia in March. After the Show, when all attempts to fly the Zodiac failed, work on five others was suspended and the licence revoked. In its place Bristol began to build a 2-seat copy of the Henry Farman biplane, which became known – quite inaccurately, since it had no boxkite features at all – as the 'Boxkite'. The first of these was flown on 29 July 1910, with a 50 h.p. Gnome engine; this remained the standard powerplant, although a few Boxkites had 50 h.p. E.N.V., 60 h.p. Renault or 70 h.p. Gnome engines. Commercially it was a great success, for it remained in production until 1914, during which time seventy-six were built, sixty-one of them with extended-span upper wings. Several were exported to Germany (two), Russia (nine), South Africa (three), Spain (two) and elsewhere. Others were built for the War Office and to equip the Bristol flying schools at Brooklands, Eastchurch and Stonehenge.

Responsibility for the Boxkite and several other early projects rested with G. H. Challenger, who with A. R. Low produced in January 1911 the company's first monoplane, a 50 h.p. single-seater with a simple undercarriage and neat appearance. Unfortunately, it was damaged on its first take-off and was not rebuilt. Five Type T biplanes were then completed, one being flown by Maurice Tabuteau in the June 1911 Circuit of Europe. Another quintet of biplanes to appear during 1911 were the austere but efficient 2-seaters designed by Eric Gordon England. On 12 April 1911 the first non-stop flight between London and Paris, on a Blériot machine, had been made by a young French monoplanist, Pierre Prier, and in June 1911 Prier came to work for the Bristol company. His first design, the P-1, was intended to compete on 1 July in the race at Eastchurch for the Gordon Bennett Cup, but could not be completed in time. Two further P-1's were built for the Circuit of Britain race, and these three monoplanes gave rise to a batch of seven single-seat military trainers and twenty-four larger 2-seaters. Of the latter, eleven had 50 h.p. Gnome engines, the rest 70 h.p. Gnomes and 1 ft. 6 in. (0·46 m.) longer fuselages. All but three had their seats in tandem.

Another new designer joined the company in January 1912 in the person of Henry Coanda (q.v.), a young French-domiciled Rumanian who had already produced some ingenious designs on the Continent. He began his career at Bristol with a few more orthodox 2-seaters, but then designed a pair of monoplanes to compete in the Military Trials at Larkhill. Powered by 80 h.p. Gnome engines, they had a wing span of 40 ft. 0 in. (12·19 m.) and a distinctive quadricycle undercarriage, and were capable of 73 m.p.h. (117 km/hr.). They shared third place in the Trials with the British-built Deperdussin and were later bought for the R.F.C. and given serial numbers 262 and 263. The War Office's monoplane ban later in 1912 eliminated any prospect of further production for the R.F.C., but a version with increased span (as illustrated) was developed for export. Twenty-one of these were completed, mostly for Italy and Rumania. From autumn 1912 Coanda produced a variety of biplane designs, including a floatplane. Most of these were 'one-off' ventures, but two were produced in quantity. The first was the B.R.7, seven of which were built, but the most successful was the T.B.8, very similar to the military monoplane. Fifty-three T.B.8's were built by Bristol, ten of the Rumanian monoplanes were also converted to T.B.8 standard, and the type was built under licence in France by Breguet. A final batch of twelve, built for the R.N.A.S. after the outbreak of World War 1, had aileron controls instead of the standard system of wing-warping.

The Bristol company's finest prewar product however was undoubtedly the Baby Biplane, later known as the Scout. It was designed by F. S. Barnwell, was completed in February 1914 and was the focus of attention at Olympia in the following month, both for its small size and for its obvious promise. Already, in trials at Larkhill, it had flown at 95 m.p.h. (153 km/hr.); when 24 ft. 7 in. (7·49 m.) wings were fitted after the Show, it reached 97·5 m.p.h. (157 km/hr.) at Farnborough on the power of its 80 h.p. Gnome, and two additional machines were laid down. These were designated Scout B and differed only in minor details such as cowling shape and wing bracing. The original machine, now known as the Scout A, was sold for £400 to Lord Carbery, who replaced the Gnome with the 80 h.p. Le Rhône engine from his Morane-Saulnier monoplane and flew it to speeds of 100 m.p.h. (161 km/hr.) and above. In July 1914 Carbery entered the Scout A in the London–Paris race, but ran out of fuel on the return journey. He ditched in the Channel, but the subsequent salvage attempt proved a failure. On the outbreak of war the two Scout B's, which had not yet flown, were impressed by the War Office, given the military serials 633 and 648* and allocated to Nos. 3 and 5 Squadrons with the R.F.C. in France.

**Caudron**  59
The brothers Gaston and René Caudron established an aeroplane factory at Romiotte (Seine) in 1910, and their little biplane exhibited later that year at the Paris *Salon* was generally regarded as one of the most progressive aircraft on display. By the outbreak of World War 1 Caudron biplanes were accepted as among the safest, simplest and least expensive aircraft so far produced in France. In its issue of 1 March 1911, *The Aero* refers to the testing of two prototypes at Issy, one (illustrated) with warp-controlled wings and the other with between-wing ailerons. On the former machine, then powered only by a 25 h.p. Anzani, Céi made one flight lasting an hour and another in which he carried a passenger, and this may have been the same Caudron that made the first night flight over Paris in February 1911.

By the time of the December 1911 *Salon* the Caudron had been de-

veloped into a somewhat larger machine, with a more powerful Anzani, a wood and fabric nacelle, extensions to the upper wings and twin rectangular rudders. Powerplants fitted to the later G.II and G.III developed versions included various Anzanis of up to 100 h.p., and Gnome, Clerget and Le Rhône rotaries of 60 or 80 h.p. The 1911/12 model soon became highly popular, especially as a school aircraft, both for its remarkably low price of £320 and for its pleasant handling qualities. One of the leading flying schools in Britain, run by W. H. Ewen at Hendon, was equipped with Caudron biplanes, and among the leading exponents of the type were F. W. Goodden (later chief test pilot of the Royal Aircraft Factory) and Sydney Pickles. Although the G.III was later to establish itself as one of the most reliable wartime training aircraft, at first it attracted more attention outside France than it did in its home country. An early customer was the Naval Wing of the R.F.C., possibly inspired by the trials of a twin-float Caudron aboard the French cruiser-turned-seaplane tender *Foudre* in 1912. At any rate, the British service ordered four Caudron floatplanes, although only one of these remained on R.N.A.S. charge at the outbreak of war. René Caudron, in 1913, demonstrated the value of photographic reconnaissance by taking aerial pictures of Peking from one of his biplanes, which resulted in a dozen machines being built for the Chinese Army. Caudron exhibits at the 1913 *Salon* included a 50 h.p.

* This corrects the information given in *Fighters 1914–19*.

Gnome amphibious version, and a pusher-engined floatplane with a 100 h.p. Gnome, but so far as is known neither of these was produced in quantity.

One other pre-war product worthy of mention was the single-seat monoplane produced by René Caudron in 1912. Ewen's school boasted two of these machines, and the first of them was flown by Maurice Guillaux in the original U.K. Aerial Derby at Hendon in June 1912. Powered by a 45 h.p. Anzani, it was one of the most attractive competitors and was surpassed in outright speed only by the Blériot 2-seater.

## Coanda   53 & 74

The activities of the talented young Rumanian designer Henry Coanda after 1911 are described under the Bristol heading, but before this Coanda had built at least two remarkable designs in France. Coanda was born in Bucharest in 1886, the son of the Rumanian Minister for War, and was educated in France, Germany and Belgium. Although he showed early promise as a sculptor, his aptitude for science and mathematics led him into a technical rather than an artistic career, and at the Berlin *Sporthalle* in December 1907 he exhibited a model of an aeroplane designed to fly by re-action propulsion.

Construction of a full-size re-action-propelled aeroplane was started by Coanda while at the *Ecole Supérieur Aéronautique* in Paris, and it was exhibited at the second *Salon de l'Aéronautique* in October

1910. It was remarkably clean aero-dynamically, though its plywood-covered steel-tube airframe was perhaps less strong than it appeared. Drag-producing interplane struts and bracing wires were reduced to an absolute minimum, and the tail was an obliquely-mounted cruci-form structure whose four triangular movable surfaces could be operated in opposing pairs to perform the functions of ailerons or in concert to act as an elevator. A 4-cylinder Clerget inline engine was mounted high in front of the pilot's seat, with multiple gears driving a centrifugal air compressor in the extreme nose. The fan was enclosed in a truncated conical fairing with an adjustable diaphragm at the front to regulate the air entry. The modest thrust which this fan could have generated would have been highly inadequate, and despite alleged descriptions of such an event it is virtually certain that the aircraft never flew. The suggestion, once made quite seri-ously, that it flew as a petrol-burning jet, can be dismissed simply by considering the location of the pilot in relation to the 'jet' efflux. A minor mystery concerns the undercarriage. As displayed at the 1910 *Salon* this was undoubtedly fixed, with a sub-stantial skid firmly attached to the yoke-shaped axle; but drawings of French origin, published a little later, show in dotted line a proposal for knuckle-jointed legs permitting the wheels to retract to lie semi-recessed in the lower wings. Investi-gation has failed to establish whether this proposal was ever put into practice. However, whatever its limitations as a practical flying machine, the Coanda was undoubtedly an ingenious and forward-looking design.

Coanda's next aeroplane, built in 1911 with an eye on the autumn *Concours Militaire*, employed a less radical, but still unorthodox, method of propulsion. It, too, was a sesquiplane, with triangular endplate stabilisers at the extremities of the lower wings, and had a circular-section fuselage terminating in a tail similar to that of the turbine machine. Power was provided by two 70 h.p. Gnome engines, mounted transversely on either side of the nose. These rotated in the line of flight, instead of at right angles to it, but did so in opposite directions to cancel the torque. An ingenious differential gear enabled either or both engines to drive the single 4-blade tractor propeller. A scale model exhibited at the December 1911 *Salon*, labelled as an exact reproduction of the *Concours* machine, revealed an increased-span lower wing and a more sophisticated finish than published photographs of the Coanda Twin under test in the summer. But the Twin was unplaced in the military competition, and at the end of the year Henry Coanda left France to join the British and Colonial Aeroplane Co. at Bristol, where he remained until September 1914.

**Cody** 16 & 17

Samuel Franklin Cody (1861–1913), an expatriate American, was kiting instructor to the Royal Engineers at the Balloon Factory, Farnborough, where at the beginning of the century he patented a Hargrave-type boxkite glider that was later adopted by the British Army. Cody was very much a rule-of-thumb designer, with no pretensions to technical expertise, but he was a natural pilot who quickly developed an instinctive feel for what was right or wrong with an aeroplane. This was founded on experience acquired during early experiments with man-carrying kites, which in 1905 led him to his first full-size aircraft, a 51 ft. 0 in. (15·54 m.) span glider biplane. Tested with moderate success at Farnborough and Crystal Palace in 1905–6, this was the first aircraft in England to be fitted with ailerons. It was followed by a powered kite with a 12 h.p. Buchet engine that made unpiloted runs along a wire at Farnborough in 1907.

At the end of 1907, Cody began to build his first full-scale man-carrying powered aeroplane, based broadly on the Wright formula but with several individual features of its own. Cody, however, employed large between-wing ailerons instead of the Wrights' wing-warping, and had a separately controlled rear rudder. Mounted centrally above the upper wings was a second rudder, and trailing behind them a large triangular fantail. The aircraft was given the official title 'British Army Aeroplane No. 1', although it was antedated by the machine already commissioned by the War Office from J. W. Dunne (*q.v.*). The airframe was completed by April 1908 and was meant to be powered by a 50 h.p. Panhard–

Levassor motor car engine. However, this failed during its preliminary tests and Cody was allowed to use instead the 50 h.p. Antoinette from the airship *Nulli Secundus I*. There is still some conflict of opinion over the first flight date of Army Aeroplane No. 1. The first fully authenticated take-off took place on 29 September 1908, when it made a hop-flight of 234 ft. (71·3 m.), but there are still those who claim that the aircraft flew in May. However, it has now been established, not only that the *Nulli Secundus* engine was not available to Cody until much later, after the airship was broken up, but that on the May date advanced by his supporters, Cody was not even *at* Farnborough. The point is somewhat academic perhaps, since Army Aeroplane No. 1 did not register a flight of any note until 16 October, when it covered 1,390 ft. (423·7 m.) before crash-landing. That flight is recognised officially as the first *sustained* powered flight made in Great Britain. At the time, Cody was still an American national; he did not acquire British citizenship until October 1909. The history of Army Aeroplane No. 1 is one of repeated trial and error, with modifications made after practically every attempt. The ailerons occupied various positions, and for a short time were discarded, as was the overhead rudder; the fore and aft booms were lengthened to give better longitudinal control; and for a while a biplane tail was carried in front of the rear rudder. In its February 1909 form (illustrated) it began to make more consistent flights, and

on 14 May covered 1 mile (1·6 km.). On 11 August it made its first flight with a new engine, a 60 h.p. E.N.V., which vastly improved the performance, and three days later Colonel Capper, the Balloon Factory's Superintendent, was taken up for the first passenger flight in a British aircraft. On 8 September it flew for more than an hour around Laffan's Plain, travelling some 40 miles (64 km.).

This and later Cody aeroplanes were noteworthy both for their size and for their robust construction. So enormous was the shed built to house Army Aeroplane No. 1 that it was nicknamed 'The Cathedral', a term which, by extension, also came to be applied to the aeroplane.* Their undoubted strength was attributable partly to Cody's natural thoroughness, but in large measure was necessitated by the hazards of Laffan's Plain as a flying ground.

In 1910 Cody produced a further biplane, similar to the final form of Army Aeroplane No. 1, in which to compete for the British Empire Michelin Trophy No. 1. After qualifying on this for his Aviator's Certificate (No. 9) in June, Cody replaced the original 60 h.p. Green with an E.N.V. of similar power, and in his first attempt set up new British records for distance and endurance by flying 94·5 miles (152·08 km.) in 2 hr. 24 min. These were short-lived, but on 31 December 1910, the very last day of the con-

---

* An alternative theory is that 'cathedral' was a popular contraction of *catahedral* – what is more usually known today as anhedral.

test, Cody re-established his title to them by flying for twice as long (4 hr. 47 min.) to cover a prize-winning distance of 185·46 miles (298·47 km.). A Green-engined development of this aircraft, with twin rudders (each with a small, fixed tailplane), was flown by Cody in the July 1911 Circuit of Britain race. He finished fourth and was the only British competitor to finish the course. In the same machine he later won both the Michelin events for 1911 and again set a new British endurance record. Re-engined with a 120 h.p. Austro-Daimler, it carried 4 passengers for 7 miles (11·25 km.) in January 1912.

For the 1912 Military Trials, Cody designed a tractor monoplane, also powered by one of the big Austro-Daimler engines. A distinctive aeroplane, it had two seats side by side in a bamboo-framed fuselage that was fabric-covered (apart from two transparent side panels) for about two-thirds of its length. Twin rudders and twin elevators, all kite-shaped, formed a 'box' at the rear, and the 43 ft. 6 in. (13·26 m.) wings were warp-controlled. It flew in June, but in July, a month before the Trials, it collided with a stray cow when landing on Laffan's Plain and was wrecked. Hastily, Cody constructed a biplane to take its place, following broadly the pattern of his 1911 Circuit machine but with extended-span wings, twin kite-shaped rudders and the engine from the crashed monoplane. It was an excellent machine of its type, but for 1912 its layout was unprogressive and outdated. By any logical system

of judging it should have taken third place behind the Hanriot and Farman entries, and was well behind the *hors concours* B.E.2. As things were judged, however, it was declared the winner of the £5,000 first prize, and two production examples (later serialled 301 and 304) were ordered for the R.F.C. The Trials machine, re-engined with a 100 h.p. Green, later brought Cody the Michelin Trophy for the third year in succession.

For the 1913 Circuit of Britain, Cody built a 60 ft. 0 in. (18·29 m.) development of the Trials biplane with a 100 h.p. Green and a single kite-shaped rudder of increased area. It was completed in mid-July with a landing gear of one large 3-step central float and a small stabilising float beneath each of the inboard strut bays. After satisfactory flotation tests it began general flight testing with a temporary wheeled undercarriage, but on 7 August it broke up in the air and Cody and his passenger were thrown out and killed. So ended, prematurely and at only the beginning of real success, the career of a gifted flier who, as *Flight* remarked, 'was of the real type of which pioneers are made'.

## Curtiss  14, 31 & 32
Before his attraction to aviation, Glenn Hammond Curtiss (1878–1930) was a leading builder and racer of motor-cycles, on one of which he established a world land speed record of 136·3 m.p.h. (219·35 km/hr.) in January 1907. Later that year he joined the Aerial Experiment Association founded by Doctor

and Mrs. Alexander Graham Bell (*see* the McCurdy entry on page 146). Curtiss' main contribution to the partnership were his Vee-type engines, which powered all four of the A.E.A. machines, but he soon emerged as a designer in his own right. The first aeroplane ascribed to Curtiss was the June Bug, the third A.E.A. type, which made its first flight at Hammondsport on 21 June 1908. On 4 July it won a prize offered by the journal *Scientific American* for the first officially recorded flight in the United States of more than 1 km. (although previous achievements by the Wrights were well in excess of this modest figure). Spanning some 46 ft. 0 in. (14·02 m.), the June Bug had the same converging aileron wingtips that characterised the earlier A.E.A. machines, weighed about 650 lb. (295 kg.) and was powered by a 40 h.p. Curtiss V-8 engine. At the end of 1908, Curtiss fitted the aircraft with pontoons and renamed it Loon, but could not persuade this primitive seaplane to leave the water.

To produce his second aeroplane, Curtiss left the A.E.A. and went into partnership with Augustus M. Herring, who in the 1890s had helped Octave Chanute to build some of his successful gliders. Together, Curtiss and Herring formed the first aircraft manufacturing company in America, and their first biplane appeared in the spring of 1909. Built for the Aeronautic Society of New York, it was broadly similar to the June Bug, but a smaller machine of some 550 lb. (250 kg.) and powered by a 4-cylinder Curtiss

engine of 30 h.p. It made its first flight at Morris Park, and Curtiss named it Gold Bug, from the yellow coloured balloon silk that covered the flying surfaces. The Gold Bug was a much more viable machine than the June Bug, the major difference being in the method of lateral control. Curtiss had become involved in a rather unsavoury legal dispute with the Wrights, who claimed infringement of their patent in wing-warping as a method of control, and so to avoid compromising the situation further Curtiss adopted, in the Gold Bug, a system using between-wing ailerons which were actuated by a shoulder yoke worn by the pilot. The Gold Bug's mainplanes were square-ended and horizontal throughout their span, instead of bowing inward towards each other at the tips like those of the June Bug.

So successful were the early trials of the Gold Bug that the Curtiss-Herring company embarked almost immediately upon a more powerful version with a 50 h.p. Curtiss V-8 engine. The Golden Flyer, as this aeroplane became known, made its debut at the *Grande Semaine d'Aviation de la Champagne* at Rheims, making its maiden flight during the meeting on 25 August 1909. Three days later, Curtiss had captured the Gordon Bennett Trophy by completing the 12·43 mile (20 km.) course in 15 min. 50·4 sec. at an average speed of 47·09 m.p.h. (75·789 km/hr.), and the following day he achieved the double by winning the *Prix de la Vitesse* at 52·63 m.p.h. (84·706 km/hr.). Even before the Rheims meeting, Curtiss had a healthy list of orders for both aeroplanes and engines, and aircraft of the Golden Flyer type featured in a number of history-making events during the next few years. Curtiss himself went on to win the speed prize at Brescia in Italy in September, and by the following summer was making a determined effort to impress the U.S. Army and Navy with the military possibilities of aeroplanes. In June he demonstrated a mock bombing attack on a dummy warship, and early in August the first air-to-ground wireless message was sent from a Curtiss machine flown by E. W. Pickerill. But the real breakthrough came on 14 November 1910, when Eugene Ely took off in a developed Golden Flyer type from a platform aboard the U.S.S. *Birmingham* in Hampton Roads, Virginia. Ely completed the sequence on 18 January 1911 when he landed on a similar platform on the afterdeck of the U.S.S. *Pennsylvania* in San Francisco Bay. On touching down the aircraft was brought to a halt by using spring hooks, fixed to the undercarriage, to engage a series of arrester cables held to the deck by sandbags. These events marked the beginnings of the aircraft carrier and of today's deck landing techniques.

They also heralded Curtiss' important contribution to the early development of waterborne aircraft. His first seaplane, flown at San Diego on 26 January 1911, was little more than a modified Golden Flyer type, mounted on a single central float, with small stabilising skid-

floats under the lower wingtips and a low-set frontal elevator. A later version had twin parallel main floats. By the end of February 1911, Curtiss had flown one of his seaplanes with a passenger on board, had developed an amphibious wheel-and-float seaplane, and had demonstrated (again on the *Pennsylvania*) how a seaplane could be lowered to the water from a warship, take off for a mission, land alongside and be winched aboard. Curtiss' demonstrations convinced the U.S. Navy, who gave him an order for an amphibious seaplane; it was eventually designated A.1 (U.S. Navy Airplane No. 1). The U.S. Army's first aircraft had been the Wright Military Flyer Type A, but here too Curtiss secured early orders. One Type D, also a development of the Golden Flyer (and sometimes called the Triad), became the Signal Corps' second aircraft, and in 1911 Curtiss delivered three Type E biplanes, which had 60 h.p. instead of 50 h.p. engines, but were otherwise similar; one of them was fitted with floats.

The next major advance in marine aircraft design came in the first Curtiss hull-type flying boat, which made its maiden flight on 10 January 1912. It still bore the outdated frontal elevator of Curtiss' earlier aeroplanes, but this feature quickly disappeared and the standard 100 h.p. Curtiss-engined 'boat of 1912–13 was a first-class aeroplane. It was adopted by the U.S. Navy with the designation C.2, and in 1912 a similar aircraft was the first to fly with the newly-invented

Sperry gyroscopic automatic pilot. A British licence to build the Curtiss flying boat was acquired by White and Thompson Ltd., the hulls being built by S. E. Saunders at Cowes. A larger, twin-engined 'boat, named *America*, was begun in 1914, and was to have been flown by the former Royal Navy pilot John C. Porte in an attempt to cross the Atlantic by stages. Two prototypes were begun, each having a wing span of 72 ft. 0 in. (21·95 m.) and two 100 h.p. Curtiss OX engines. The outbreak of war prevented the attempt from being made, but the two prototypes were later purchased by the British Admiralty and, under Porte's direction, were developed into the excellent Felixstowe flying boats of wartime fame (see *Bombers 1914–19*).

## de Havilland  8, 66 & 68

Geoffrey de Havilland shares with A. V. Roe the dominant position among British pioneer airmen. Roe's successes up to 1914 were greater, but in some respects de Havilland was the more versatile of the two. His active interest in aviation stemmed from an early association with F. T. Hearle, who collaborated in the construction of de Havilland's first aeroplane in 1909. The end product did not have an entirely orthodox appearance, although in designing it de Havilland attempted no radical departure from contemporary design practices. The machine's most individual feature was its propulsion system: the 'flat four' engine, designed by de Havilland and built for him by the Iris Motor Company, drove two aluminium pusher propellers by means of a bevel gear and the radiator was mounted above it, horizontally, in the centre-section gap between the two upper wing halves. The biplane was taken in November 1909 to Beacon Hill, Hampshire, where it was assembled and prepared for its first flight. This was attempted in the early weeks of 1910, but after running for some 40 yd. downhill it rose steeply, travelling a similar distance through the air before the left wing crumpled and the aircraft fell heavily to the ground. No subsequent attempt was made to rebuild the machine. The cause of the crash was attributed to the softness of the wood and the inadequacy of the cross-sections employed in its construction.

de Havilland's second biplane, also designed in association with Frank Hearle, was more successful. It used the engine salvaged from the wreck of the first machine, this time directly driving a 2-blade mahogany propeller. The wings had larger ailerons, mounted behind the trailing edge, the rudder was enlarged and one-piece front and rear elevators were fitted. Spruce, ash and hickory were used to make the airframe stronger, and the flying surfaces were covered with calico and specially treated with Pegamoid. The aircraft weighed about 1,100 lb. (500 kg.) and had a wing span of 33 ft. 6 in. (10·21 m.). It was flown at Beacon Hill in September 1910, and before long de Havilland was taking up Hearle or members of his own family in the passenger seat. Completing and testing this machine had all but exhausted de Havilland's modest resources, but he was able to persuade His Majesty's Balloon Factory at Farnborough to give him a job as a designer and test pilot and to buy the biplane for £400. It proved itself to the War Office's satisfaction with a one-hour endurance flight early in 1911, and, since it followed the basic layout of the current Henry Farman biplanes, was given the 'Farman Experimental' designation F.E. 1 as the first aircraft owned by the Factory. It continued to be flown for some time, with minor mishaps, and was later given a biplane tail to eliminate a tendency towards tail-heaviness. Eventually, while being flown by Lieutenant Ridge, the Factory's Assistant Superintendent, it crashed due to a crankshaft failure in the Iris engine. The wreckage was salvaged and rebuilt into the F.E. 2, with a 50 h.p. Gnome engine, and later still as a single-float seaplane.

In 1910 the Balloon Factory was officially denied the power to create its own aeroplanes, but its Superintendent, Mervyn O'Gorman, circumvented this in characteristic fashion by securing, in January 1911, permission for the terms of repair work to include reconstruction as well. The Factory staff then interpreted this approval so freely that they had virtual liberty to put into practice their own ideas for aircraft design. Their first chance came when a Blériot tractor monoplane was sent to Farnborough for repair. de Havilland wanted to rebuild this as a tractor biplane, but on advice from O'Gorman he turned it in-

stead into a canard pusher type along similar lines to Santos-Dumont's 14bis of 1906, and the aircraft was labelled S.E.1 (Santos Experimental No. 1). The redesign was undertaken by de Havilland with F. M. Green (who had been mainly responsible for his coming to Farnborough), and by the time they had finished, virtually all that remained of the original Blériot was its 60 h.p. E.N.V. engine. This was mounted in the central nacelle, in front of the pilot's cockpit, with a chain drive to the 2-blade pusher propeller. Twin rear booms supported the tail unit with its two rudders, and the wing span of the S.E.1 was 38 ft. 0 in. (11·58 m.). de Havilland began flight testing the S.E.1 in June 1911. Two months later Lieutenant Ridge, still a relatively inexperienced pilot, insisted on flying it, but got into difficulties that he was unable to handle. The S.E.1 went into a spin and crashed, and Ridge was killed.

The second metamorphosis wrought by de Havilland and Green followed the acquisition of a Voisin biplane, formerly owned by the Duke of Westminster. This reappeared, as the B.E.1, for its first flight on 1 January 1912, and as *Flight* wryly commented afterwards 'It seemed to us that there was more remodelling than anything else'. de Havilland had got his wish to design a tractor biplane, and all that remained from the original Voisin were the 60 h.p. Wolseley engine, its fuel tank, radiator and a few minor fittings. (The letters in its official designation signified Blériot

Experimental, indicating simply that it was of tractor configuration.) Compared with the open-exhaust rotary engines then in common use, the Vee-type Wolseley was so quiet that the B.E.1 was referred to as 'the Army's silent aeroplane'. Later on even the engine was replaced, by a 60 h.p. Renault. During a useful life of some 3½ years, the B.E.1 was probably the first aircraft to be issued with a basic certificate of airworthiness, and took part in some of the earliest experiments in the use of airborne wireless equipment. In the summer of 1912 it was taken on charge by the R.F.C. and given the serial number 201. In February 1912 a similar machine, the B.E.2, was completed, having a 70 h.p. Renault engine and (later) the R.F.C. serial 202. In May the War Office ordered four B.E.2-type aircraft from Vickers, and in August the original B.E.2 was flown *hors concours* in many events at the Military Trials. Official winner of the competition was Cody's Army Aeroplane No. 1, but the B.E.2 eclipsed it completely, setting up in the process a new British altitude record of 10,560 ft. (3,219 m.) on 12 August. As ultimately developed, the B.E.2 type became the world's first aircraft to attain full inherent stability.

Geoffrey de Havilland also played a leading part in the design of later B.E. types at Farnborough, but of far greater historical significance was the little B.S.1 (Blériot Scout) of 1912, the true progenitor of the single-seat fighter. Intended to provide some of the answers to high speed flight problems, the B.S.1 was originally meant to have a 140 h.p. Gnome engine and reach a speed of 90 m.p.h. (144·8 km/hr.). As built, it recorded a maximum of 91·7 m.p.h. (147·6 km/hr.) with a Gnome of only 100 h.p. Detail design was carried out from August 1912, and de Havilland piloted the B.S.1 on its first flight in February 1913. The aircraft had a rate of climb from sea level of 900 ft/min. (4·57 m/sec.), a landing speed of 49 m.p.h. (78·8 km/hr.), and its performance was highly satisfactory in most respects. The rudder, however, was too small to give adequate directional control. de Havilland ordered a larger rudder, but in March 1913, before this could be fitted, the B.S.1 went into a flat spin and was wrecked. Later in the year it was rebuilt with an 80 h.p. Gnome engine, split elevators, small triangular fin surfaces above and below the rear fuselage and a larger, ear-shaped rudder. In this form it was known briefly as the B.S.2 and subsequently as the S.E.2 – the initials this time standing for Scout Experimental. Its subsequent career is detailed in the *Fighters 1914–19* volume.

## Denhaut/Donnet-Lévêque 33

On 15 March 1912 the pilot-engineer F. Denhaut took off from the Seine at Juvisy in a flying-boat of his own design – the first of its kind in Europe. The flight nearly ended in tragedy, but Denhaut survived to rebuild the machine, incorporating many points gleaned from a study of the American Curtiss machines, and on 13 April he made more than half a dozen water take-offs and landings without further incident. A 2-seater with a 50 h.p. Gnome rotary engine, the Denhaut flying boat attracted the attention of MM. Donnet and Lévêque, who shortly afterwards established a company to build and market it. Premises were acquired at Quay de Seine, Argenteuil, and among the other executives were Denhaut and the celebrated competition flier Lieutenant de Vaisseau Conneau, better known by his pseudonym of André Beaumont.

The first two Donnet-Lévêque 'boats were completed under Denhaut's direction at Juvisy and flown to Argenteuil on 26 July 1912 by Beaumont. On 9 August, Beaumont set out on an attempted flight from Paris to London, calling at various other towns en route; but a take-off accident at Boulogne prematurely ended his attempt. However, he made up for his disappointment by winning the King of Belgium's prize for seaplanes on 6–7 September, when the aircraft proved entirely reliable. The highly polished Donnet-Lévêque Type A exhibited at the Paris *Salon* in October 1912 revealed one major design improvement: it was now amphibious, having a twin-wheel land undercarriage which could be wound up above water level when not required.

First positive interest in the Donnet-Lévêque came from Britain, whence Vickers' pilot Archibald Low travelled to Argenteuil to try out the machine. He was not over-enthusiastic, claiming that the narrow hull and the high position of the underwing floats caused the aircraft to lack control on the water. Nevertheless, one example was ordered by the Admiralty for the R.N.A.S. station at Eastchurch. Powered by an 80 h.p. Gnome engine (which alternated with the 50 h.p. unit as the standard installation), it was delivered to Sheerness on 20 December 1912 and was given the number 18 in the first block of military serials to be allocated to British Naval aircraft. During 1912–13, Donnet-Lévêques were also supplied to the navies of Austro-Hungary (three), Denmark (two) and Sweden (one). At the beginning of 1913 Donnet left the company, which took the new name Hydro-aéroplanes Lévêque for a short while until, in association with Louis Schreck, it became Franco-British Aviation with a new base at Vernon (Eure). Donnet and Denhaut came together again in a new partnership at Île de la Jatte, and both companies subsequently produced flying boats used extensively during World War 1; the F.B.A. Type H was probably the most widely employed flying boat of the entire war period.

The Denhaut/Donnet-Lévêque design, although 'borrowing' from Curtiss early in its career, established the classic flyingboat layout of the fuselage-hull (as opposed to just a nacelle) with upswept rear end supporting the tail, and the later Curtiss 'boats in their turn benefited from the design trends indicated by the French machines.

**Deperdussin** 51 & 57

The first product of the Société Pour les Appareils Deperdussin to claim widespread attention was the Type B single-seater which appeared in 1911, the year following the formation of the company. Powered by a 50 h.p. Gnome engine, it was a neat, slender monoplane capable of 56 m.p.h. (90 km/hr.), and no less than seven Deperdussins were entered for the Circuit of Europe race that began in June. Third place in the race went to the Deperdussin flown by René Vidart. A 2-seat variant with a 100 h.p. Gnome appeared later in the year, and both types became popular in France and Britain. Leading British exponents included James Valentine, W. H. Ewen and Captain Patrick Hamilton; another was Lieutenant J. C. Porte, R.N., later the pilot for the British Deperdussin Company, formed to build and market the French aircraft in Britain.

The Deperdussin's performance in the *Concours Militaire*, held at Rheims in October/November 1911, resulted in four being ordered by the French government, and in April 1912 another was delivered to the Royal Navy air station at Eastchurch. Three Deperdussins were entered for the British Military Trials in August 1912. Two of these were British-built; one (with 100 h.p. Anzani) was flown by Porte and the other, a standard Gnome-engined model, was taken over by Gordon Bell after its original pilot, the celebrated Jules Védrines, was called back to France. The best perform-ance in the Trials, however, came from Maurice Prévost, whose Gnome-engined Deperdussin was awarded the £2,000 second prize. Prior to the outbreak of war, nine Deperdussins were listed among the initial batch of R.F.C. serial number allocations, and a further five by the R.F.C.'s Naval Wing (later the R.N.A.S.).

By far the most outstanding pro-ducts of the Deperdussin company, however, were the single-seat racing monoplanes of 1912–13. Late in 1911 the ideas of the Swedish en-gineer Ruchonnet, for a monocoque fuselage shell of moulded plywood, were applied by Armand Deper-dussin's designer, Louis Béchereau, in the evolution of a small single-seater which, apart from its warp-controlled wings, was a highly ad-vanced design as well as an ex-tremely handsome one. In its original form the aircraft was powered by a semi-cowled two-row Gnome of 100 h.p., consisting of two standard 50 h.p. rotary units on a common crankshaft bearing. The wings, which were inversely tapered on the inboard trailing edges, had a span of 22 ft. 11½ in. (7·00 m.) and an area of 107·64 sq. ft. (10·00 sq. m.); overall length was 20 ft. 6 in. (6·25 m.). A twin-wheel undercarriage with a central skid was fitted. From the start the new machine was outstanding, shattering all the national speed records for distances between 5 and 150 km. (3 and 93 miles). In de-veloped form, with a simplified undercarriage and 140 h.p. Gnome, its first international honours came in Chicago on 9 September 1912, when Védrines flew the monoplane to success in the race for the Gordon Bennett Trophy at a record speed of 108·18 m.p.h. (174·01 km/hr.). Maurice Prévost re-entered the scene as pilot of the floatplane version, the winner of the first Schneider Trophy meeting held at Monaco on 15 April 1913. The Deperdussin's official winning speed of 45·75 m.p.h. (73·63 km/hr.) may seem remarkably low in relation to the 160 h.p. Gnome with which the machine was now fitted, but is explained by the fact that Prévost failed to cross the finishing line in a manner acceptable to the judges, who made him take off and fly the final 10 km. (6·21 mile) lap again. (A somewhat academic point, since all but one of the other competitors had either retired or been eliminated.) Prévost's actual average for the statutory 28 laps was about 61 m.p.h. (98 km/hr.). A 100 h.p. British-built Deperdussin floatplane was displayed at Olympia in February 1913, but the British company – no doubt affected by the War Office ban on monoplanes – was not doing well, and went into liquidation the following autumn.

The peak of the Deperdussin racer's career was reached on 29 September 1913, when it successfully defended its tenure of the Gordon Bennett Trophy at Rheims against another strong French competitor, the Pagny-designed Ponnier monoplane, a development of the Hanriot racer. Streamlining of the aircraft had now reached a high degree of finesse, with the Gnome engine fully cowled, a faired head-rest behind the pilot's seat, and other detail refinements. Three Deperdussins were entered for the race, two with 160 h.p. Gnomes and the third with a Le Rhône rotary of similar power. The day before the race, Béchereau cropped about 2 ft. 1½ in. (0·65 m.) off the wings of Prévost's Gnome-engined machine to make it faster, and it won the event with a magnificent average of 124·6 m.p.h. (200·5 km/hr.). During the event Prévost broke the existing world speed record several times, finally setting a new figure of 126·7 m.p.h. (203·85 km/hr.), the first time it had exceeded 200 km/hr. Prévost was run a close second by Jules Védrines' brother Emile, whose course average in the Ponnier monoplane was 122·7 m.p.h. (197·5 km/hr.). Because the race was flown around a circuit course, it was argued by many that the Ponnier was actually the faster machine, Prévost having won by virtue of his skilful cornering. The two aircraft were never matched over a straight course, so the issue remained undecided; but it is fair to suppose that both would have had an outright speed of some 135 m.p.h. (217 km/hr.), making them, with the Royal Aircraft Factory's S.E.4 (q.v.), the fastest aircraft in the world prior to the outbreak of war.

Unfortunately, the successes of the Deperdussin were not matched by orders for production aircraft, and in 1913 Armand Deperdussin was arrested for large-scale embezzlement. The company was taken over in 1914 by Louis Blériot, who retained Béchereau as chief designer and renamed it Société Provisoire des Aéroplanes Deperdussin. The initials were perpetuated in its successor, the Société Pour l'Aviation et ses Dérivés, from which emanated the famous wartime Spad fighters.

## Dunne 28, 29 & 30

Late in 1905 Lieutenant John William Dunne (1875–1949), formerly of the Wiltshire Regiment, was appointed as a kite designer at the Balloon Factory, Farnborough, where he was a contemporary of S. F. Cody (q.v.). Already the question of natural stability in aircraft had engaged his attention, and at Farnborough he was allowed to try out some of his ideas in the form of paper models. Colonel J. E. Capper, the Factory's Superintendent, soon obtained permission for Dunne to embark upon a full-size machine, and designs for both a monoplane and a biplane were drawn up. Work on these proceeded under conditions of great secrecy, and in 1907 they were taken to Blair Atholl, Perthshire, to be assembled and tested. Here they were camouflaged from inquisitive eyes by having white stripes and dark patches painted on their upper surfaces.

The essence of these and all other Dunne designs lay in the wing configuration, which consisted of constant-chord mainplanes swept back in an arrowhead planform. Neither the monoplane D.1 nor the 4-bay D.3 biplane had either fixed or movable vertical surfaces. The unpowered D.1 was launched from a 4-wheel trolley chassis for its first

take-off in 1907 with Colonel Capper aboard. However, when it was damaged in a crash-landing further tests were abandoned in favour of the D.3 'hang-glider', which was felt to be a safer proposition. Piloted by Lieutenant Lancelot Gibbs, the D.3 was launched from a similar trolley gear, but was wrecked when it rolled off the chassis.

Dunne's first powered machine was the D.4, a strengthened and modified development of the D.3 with a short nacelle for the pilot, fixed vertical fins between the upper and lower wingtips, and a sprung, 4-wheel undercarriage. Like its predecessors, the D.4 was camouflaged. Initially the D.4 was fitted with two 15 h.p. Buchet engines, but these developed only a fraction of their stated power. Substitution of a single 25 h.p. R.E.P. engine improved matters only slightly. Dunne himself regarded the D.4 as 'more of a hopper than a flier', and its best effort was a mere 120 ft. (36·58 m.) on 10 December 1908.

In the spring of 1909, War Office support for aeroplane development was withdrawn, and Dunne left the Balloon Factory, taking the D.4 with him. His work continued under the aegis of the Blair Atholl Aeroplane Syndicate Ltd., formed in 1910 by the Marquis of Tullibardine (heir to the Duke of Atholl), and his next aeroplane, the D.5, was built at Leysdown for the Syndicate by the Short brothers. It proved to be the first really practical aircraft designed by Dunne, making its first flight at Eastchurch on 11 March 1910 and a 2¼ mile (3½ km.) flight some two months later. It was also a passenger-carrying machine, having seats for two in a lengthened nacelle at the rear of which was mounted the 60 h.p. engine – originally an E.N.V. Type F, later a Green. Hinged ailerons were inset at the upper wingtips. The D.5 continued to make consistent flights during 1910, but early in 1911 was wrecked while being flown by an incautious pilot.

A brief monoplane interlude occurred during 1911, the D.7 'Auto-Safety Plane' shown at Olympia in March being a completion by Shorts of the rebuilding (initiated by Capper) of the D.1 glider into a 50 h.p. Gnome-engined machine with much simplified wing bracing. The wide-track wheel-and-skid undercarriage was reminiscent of the Farman 'Longhorn' – though, of course, without the latter's forward elevator. The D.7 began flight testing at Eastchurch in June, and in January 1912 Dunne flew it 'hands off' in a convincing demonstration of its stability. The D.6 was a similar but slightly larger single-seat monoplane with a 60 h.p. Green pusher engine; later it was converted to a 2-seater with a 70 h.p. Gnome.

In 1912 the remnants of the D.5 were utilised in building the D.8, the last and most successful of Dunne's stable biplanes. A single pusher propeller replaced the chain-driven pair used in the earlier designs, the ailerons were enlarged and fitted at all four wingtips, and a longer nacelle projected ahead of the centre-section Vee. The 50 h.p. Gnome of the original D.8 was re-placed later by an 80 h.p. unit, except for one machine in which a 60 h.p. Green was installed. The first D.8 was flown in June 1912, and soon attracted interest from France. After inspecting it at Eastchurch on behalf of the Nieuport company, Commandant Félix flew the French Army an 80 h.p. D.8 to Paris and thence to Villacoublay. There he gave an outstanding demonstration which included allowing the aircraft to fly itself while he climbed out on to the wing to illustrate how perfectly stable it was. A Nieuport-Dunne D.8 with simplified undercarriage was displayed at the Paris *Salon* in December. In March 1913 the British War Office ordered two 2-seat, 80 h.p. D.8's for the R.F.C. These were due for delivery in August, but by November were still uncompleted. They do not appear among the known serial number allocations to early Army aeroplanes, and presumably were never delivered. Dunne's final British design, the D.9, was a failure.

The exploits of Commandant Félix had attracted the attention of the American manufacturer W. Starling Burgess, who obtained a licence to build and develop Dunne-type aircraft in the U.S.A. Among the early Burgess-Dunnes were tandem 2-seat seaplanes with open seats; one of these became Canada's first military aeroplane, delivered in the early autumn of 1914, and the U.S. Navy's AH-7 (illustrated) was generally similar. Later Burgess-Dunnes included the staggered-wing AH-10, the private-owner Model BD, and the BDF flying boat for military reconnaissance. These were wartime products, but in May 1914 chronic ill-health had forced John Dunne to retire from an active part in aeronautical affairs, although he remained available to the War Office in a consultant capacity for the duration of hostilities.

## Ellehammer   75 & 76

Jacob Christian Hansen Ellehammer was born in 1871 at Bakkebølle in southern Zealand, the son of a former ship's carpenter, and had a typical boyhood interest in kite-flying. After an early apprenticeship to a watchmaker, he qualified in electro-mechanics and served a term as an electrician in the Royal Danish Navy. He set up his own business in 1896, and his mechanical ability involved him in such turn-of-the-century innovations as phonographs, telephones, X-ray apparatus and the cinematograph. He also designed his own internal combustion engine, and the Elleham motor-cycle, one of the first such vehicles to appear in Denmark.

There can have been few pioneers of aviation with such a diversity of talents – during his lifetime Ellehammer took out some four hundred different patents – but his very versatility was probably the reason why his aeroplanes, in their historical context, were not more significant. They appear to have satisfied Ellehammer's own expectations, but their overall contribution to world aviation progress was minimal. Nevertheless, such success as they did achieve was reached without dependence on a knowledge of

the work of other aviators. The first full-size machine (Ellehammer I) was completed at Copenhagen in 1905 after its inventor had made preliminary studies of bird flight and conducted tests with models, and was powered by a 9 h.p. 3-cylinder radial engine also designed by Ellehammer. Ellehammer was given the use of the tiny island of Lindholm, where the tractor monoplane was reassembled in a workshop and hangar erected by Ellehammer, his brother Vilhelm and cousin Lars. The island was too small to attempt a straight flight, and so a circular track some 33 ft. (10 m.) in diameter was beaten out, with a mast in the centre to which the aeroplane was tethered. Testing the Ellehammer I on its circular track eliminated the need to give it directional or lateral control – it had a fixed rudder – and centrifugal force contributed to its performance; thus, on its first attempt, on 14 January 1906, the aeroplane (without a pilot) just rose clear of the ground, and a few days later Ellehammer wrote to a local newspaper 'I regard the experiments as fully conclusive. Everything far exceeded our expectations. It was not the intention that the apparatus should go up, but when we set it going it rose and responded in every way.' Longitudinal control of the aircraft was effected by Ellehammer's 'pendulum' system, whereby the frame supporting the engine and the pilot's seat, which was suspended from the upper half-hoop framework, could be rocked to and fro to raise or lower the rear elevator. The

Ellehammer I had a wing area of 161·46 sq. ft. (15 sq. m.) and weighed 276 lb. (125 kg.). Following the early 1906 tests, Ellehammer decided to try a larger engine, and developed his little radial until it produced 20 h.p., but it was now too powerful for the original airframe, and so a series of design changes was conducted during the summer. At first, a rigid upper wing was added; then the semi-cylindrical centre-section of the original wing was removed and replaced with a flat section. An additional section was then placed along the leading edge, so that the propeller had to be moved further forward. Finally, a sail-like arrangement was adopted for the upper wing, which was now secured at the tips and centre only. This 'semi-biplane', as the Ellehammer II is usually described, was tested tethered on 16 August 1906; the next day, after modifying the engine gearing and eliminating 13¼ lb. (6 kg.) of surplus weight, Ellehammer recorded a speed of 35½ m.p.h. (57 km/hr.) around the now concreted track. Testing continued during August; on 5 September, ribs were added to the upper wing, and on 12 September the first really significant – though still tethered – flight was made, a distance through the air of 138 ft. (42 m.) being recorded.

Ellehammer was now keen to develop an aeroplane capable of making a free take-off and flying in a straight line, and so transferred his experiments to the outskirts of Copenhagen. He soon abandoned the semi-biplane for a triplane de-sign, to get more lift, and at the same time continued to develop the power of the engine. The Ellehammer III triplane was completed with the 20 h.p. 3-cylinder unit at first, but this was quickly replaced by a 5-cylinder radial developing 35 h.p. Otherwise, apart from its third lifting surface, the 1907 triplane differed in few major respects from the 1906 machine. It still had no proper means of lateral control, and the only 'rudder' surface was that obtained by fixing a fabric shield over the rear landing wheel. Ellehammer claims to have made some two hundred hop-flights in this machine before abandoning it with the admission that the third wing gave no worthwhile advantages. Hans Grade, Germany's first aviator, made some brief hops at Magdeburg in January 1909 in a triplane based on Elle-hammer's design.

The 5-cylinder engine also powered the Ellehammer IV tractor biplane of 1908, in which its designer made the first powered hop-flight in Germany in June. Two flights, each lasting 11 seconds, were made at Kiel, for which Elle-hammer received a prize of 5,000 M. The longest recorded flight by this machine, of 558 ft. (170 m.), occured on 14 January 1908. The Ellehammer V, a seaplane based on the 1908 biplane, did not fly, though it completed successful taxy-ing trials on Kalvebod Strand, near Copenhagen, and had conventional tail control surfaces and a frontal elevator. The Ellehammer VI, which its designer called the Standard, was a tractor monoplane of the Blériot type. It was powered by a 40 h.p. two-row radial engine, consisting of two of the 3-cylinder units driven from a common crankcase, had the pendulum-type elevator control and wing-warping. Count Moltke was to pilot the Standard in an attempt to be the first to cross Copenhagen Sound by aeroplane, but another aviator accomplished the flight before him and the Standard was never flown.

Ellehammer then abandoned aeroplane development due to lack of financial support, though he continued to experiment with helicopters and with the development of aero-engines. Despite his mechanical background, most of his designs were evolved by rule-of-thumb methods and intuition; but one cannot resist the speculation that, had his many talents been directed by a greater single-mindedness of purpose, Jacob Ellehammer might have ranked with the great pioneers of flying in Europe.

## Esnault-Pelterie 48

Robert Esnault-Pelterie (1881–1957), an extremely able technician, was one of the few early European pioneers able to bring the benefits of a sound engineering education to bear upon the problems associated with powered flight. Unfortunately, his early work was based on false assumptions that guided it in unprofitable directions, or he might have exerted a greater influence than he did. Though his aeroplanes, in themselves, were not especially remarkable, Esnault-Pelterie pro-

duced competently designed aero-engines, and contributed a number of 'fringe benefits' to aviation progress. Among the latter were the first hydraulically operated wheel brakes (fitted to the R.E.P.2 monoplane), the use of a single column to govern both the wing and elevator controls, the evolution of the first seat belt (1911) and, in the same year, some of the first rudimentary stress tests, effected by inverting the aeroplane and loading the wings with sandbags to prove them strong enough for flight.

Before 1908, when the Wright brothers' biplanes were demonstrated in France, there was widespread disbelief among European aviators that the Americans were so far ahead of them in the new science of aeronautics. One of the foremost sceptics was Esnault-Pelterie, who in 1904 sought to prove what he believed (or wished to believe) by building a replica of the Wrights' 1902 glider. Unfortunately, he did so with incomplete data and without appreciating the cardinal fact that the instability of the Wright machine was deliberate and an essential reason for its success. Not surprisingly, the French copy was a failure. A second machine was built, but instead of a wing-warping system (which Esnault-Pelterie considered dangerous) it had a small, independent horizontal surface to the rear of each wingtip. These could operate differentially to perform the functions of ailerons – the first time ailerons had ever been fitted to a full-size aircraft – or in concert to serve as elevators, and may be regarded as the first serious attempt to achieve lateral control by means of an aileron system; but no flights of any significance were made by this second glider.

By the time he produced his first powered aeroplane, in 1907, Esnault-Pelterie had evidently not learnt much better, for although the wings were made to warp they did so only in a downward direction. Moreover, because of its very short fuselage and lack of a vertical fin or rudder the R.E.P.1 had very poor longitudinal and directional control. The 31 ft. 6 in. (9.60 m.) wings, rigged with slight anhedral, had a lifting area of 193.57 sq. ft. (18 sq. m.), and the aircraft was powered by a 30 h.p. semi-radial engine designed by Esnault-Pelterie. Technical refinements included the use of steel tube as well as wood in the airframe construction, and the complete covering-in of the fuselage. But the engine cooling system was unsatisfactory, and the aircraft's basic lack of balance enabled it to fly no more than 1,968 ft. (600 m.) in the best of the five flights attempted in November/December 1907.

The next series of flights, which began at Buc on 8 June 1908, were made with the R.E.P.2, a considerably refined and more realistic machine with a huge trapezoidal fin and rudder and an enlarged tailplane. The wings were still warp-controlled, but reduced slightly in span and area; small auxiliary elevators, fixed on the lower front of the fuselage, were later discarded. The R.E.P.2 flew at least twice the distance of the R.E.P.1, and was able to reach a speed of over 50 m.p.h. (80 km/hr.) and a height of 98 ft (30 m.). It was still basically unstable, however, and early in 1909 was again modified, into the R.E.P.2bis, with a balanced rudder, the elevator mounted further aft and the wing area reduced to 169.53 sq. ft. (15.75 sq. m.) by the simple expedient of removing the inboard wing ribs and their covering. In this form it flew again on 15 February 1909, and throughout the spring and summer made numerous flights of consistent duration, the best being one of 5 miles (8 km.) on 22 May. At the Rheims meeting that August four R.E.P. monoplanes were entered, but only the R.E.P.2bis succeeded in taking off. During the year the R.E.P.2bis was displayed at the Olympia and Paris exhibitions, where it was optimistically offered for sale at £1,400.

Esnault-Pelterie continued during the next 3-4 years to develop his monoplane ideas, which were eventually rationalised in more orthodox machines such as the Types D (60 h.p. R.E.P.) and K (80 h.p. Gnome), having conventional undercarriages and carrying a passenger. One such model was the subject of licence production by Vickers (q.v.), while in December 1910, R.E.P. Type D's set speed records (with a passenger) over 100 km. and 250 km. courses. A creditable performance was returned by an R.E.P. monoplane which competed in the June 1911 Circuit of Europe. The rules of this event permitted pilots to change their mounts en route, but Gibert, flying the R.E.P., was the only monoplane pilot to finish using the same machine throughout, and was placed fifth in the final results. The French and Turkish air forces employed R.E.P. monoplanes prior to World War 1, and a few R.E.P. parasol-winged monoplanes were in French and R.N.A.S. service during the early part of the war; one of the latter, which crashed in Holland, was used by the *Luchtvaart Afdeling*. By this time, however, Esnault-Pelterie had forsaken aircraft production for an even more challenging venture: the study of rocket propulsion and the exciting prospect of space travel.

## Etrich    40

The first aeronautical experiments by the Austrian engineer Doktor Igo Etrich were made in 1904, in association with Franz Wels. Their first flying machine was a model of a tail-less glider, with which a number of tests were conducted, leading to a full-size, man-carrying glider flown at Oberalstadt, Bohemia, in 1907. This, too, was of the 'flying wing' type, with echoes of the Lilienthal gliders and a superficial resemblance to the Vuia monoplane (*q.v.*). Subsequent attempts at powered machines, using a 24 h.p. Antoinette engine, brought little success until 1909, when Etrich (working now without Wels) fitted his aircraft with a rudder and a frontal elevator.

Etrich's name is, however, associated indissolubly with the *Taube*

monoplane, surely one of the most bird-like aeroplanes ever created. He was probably influenced by Blériot (and thence indirectly by Vuia) in electing to follow a tractor monoplane layout; but curiously enough, despite its name (meaning 'Dove') and bird-like looks, the shape of its wings was based on the winged seed of the *Zanonia Macrocarpa* palm tree, which Etrich considered to have ideal aerodynamic qualities. An earlier machine constructed along these lines flew at Wiener-Neustadt in November 1909, subsequently achieving speeds up to 43 m.p.h. (70 km/hr.) and flights nearly 3 miles (4·75 km.) in length. From results with this aircraft Etrich designed the *Taube*, whose prototype appeared in 1910. In flight, the *Taube's* graceful outline aptly justified its name, although in close-up the aeroplane was smothered in a profusion of pylons, kingposts, warping and bracing wires, undercarriage struts and a long support bar beneath the wings with a small outrigger wheel at each end. Wing-warping was controlled by a wheel in the pilot's cockpit, the tail controls being operated by foot pedals.

The original *Taube* had a 120 h.p. Austro-Daimler engine, but after Etrich concluded a licence agreement with the Rumpler Flugzeug-Werke of Johannisthal most early *Tauben* were fitted with 100 or 120 h.p. Mercedes units. Subsequently, after a dispute with Rumpler, Etrich relinquished his copyright in the design, with the result that at least nine other German manufacturers produced *Tauben* of one kind or another; those built by D.F.W. and Jeannin had steel-tube fuselage frames and were known as *Stahltauben*. Before World War I, *Tauben* were built to the requirements of individual private customers and, from 1912–13, by so many different manufacterers for military purposes, that no two versions were absolutely alike. Generally speaking, engines of 100 to 120 h.p. were the norm, and performance variations were marginal; the differences were mainly dimensional. The figures quoted on page 56 are for a typical Rumpler-built *Taube*; for another version, *The Aero* of 30 November 1910 quoted a wing span of 44 ft. 11 in. (13·70 m.) and length of 34 ft. 10 in. (10·62 m.); while *Flight* of 11 November 1911 illustrated a still larger *Taube* of 48 ft. 0 in. (14·63 m.) span and 37 ft. 0 in. (11·28 m.) length. The early products of the Albatros (*q.v.*) company were particularly influenced by the *Taube* design.

Ultimate production of *Tauben* reached about five hundred; most of these were for military purposes, their wartime career being described in the *Fighters 1914–19* volume in this series. Other ingenious but less successful designs by Igo Etrich between 1910 and 1913 included a crescent-winged machine and a *Taube*-type 'limousine' monoplane. The latter, which seated four people, had a high wing and bulbous front fuselage liberally provided with windows affording an excellent view outward and downward from the cabin.

**Fabre** 1

Henri Fabre, the pioneer of the hydroplane, was born near Marseille in 1882 of a family of shipowners, a background whose influence was evident in both the design and the control system of his successful *hydravions* of 1910–11. After qualifying as an engineer, he began in 1905 to study the works of Blériot, Ferber, Voisin and other French air pioneers, and later began to carry out selected experiments in aerodynamics; in 1909 he designed and built his first seaplane, a triple-float machine with three Anzani engines driving a single propeller. This aeroplane did not fly, but later the same year Fabre began to build a second machine which was to be successful.

The new aircraft was powered by a single Gnome 7-cylinder rotary engine, and was one of the first machines to use this new powerplant created in 1909 by the Seguin brothers. The Fabre seaplane was a frail, ungainly affair, and scarcely deserves to be called a practical aeroplane, but it is significant historically as the first seaplane to make a successful flight, preceding the American Curtiss by a year. Fabre chose a canard layout, the monoplane wing being at the rear with the engine installed behind it driving a two-blade Chauvière propeller. The wings had a single main spar of a novel lattice-girder construction that was both strong and aerodynamically efficient. Fabre's nautical thinking was reflected in the technique of covering the wings, whose canvas could be reefed up to the spar during storage or for protective or repair purposes. For flight, it was stretched out over the ribs and held taut by fastening it to each rib end with a sprung hook. Lateral control of the machine was effected by wing-warping. The aircraft's 'fuselage' consisted simply of two girders, built to the same lattice-type construction as the wing spar but boxed in. A tiller-type control rod attached to each rudder gave the machine directional control through the air.

On 28 March 1910 – never having flown in his life before, even as a passenger – Henri Fabre essayed his first take-off from the harbour at La Mède, near Marseille. On the first attempt the aircraft hydroplaned across the water at some 55 km/hr. (34 m.p.h.) but did not rise into the air. On the second attempt, however, after a run of some 300 m. (984 ft.), Fabre took off and made a flight of about 500 m. (1,640 ft.) some 2 m. (6·5 ft.) above the surface. On his fifth flight, made on the following day, he covered a distance of some 6 km. (3·75 miles), and several subsequent flights were made, proving the aircraft to be a particularly stable design. It came to grief on 18 May 1910 when, after having flown to an altitude of about 20 m. (65·5 ft.) it came down to land at too high a speed and was seriously damaged. Among the spectators on this occasion was Louis Paulhan, with whom Fabre had hoped to go into partnership. Such an alliance did not materialise, but Paulhan's own biplane of 1911 (q.v.) featured a similar type of wing spar construction to the Fabre machine.

By October 1910, when the seaplane was exhibited in Paris, Fabre had rebuilt it, incorporating a number of alterations. Believing the original design to be too stable, he doubled the area of the forward lower lifting surface and replaced the aerofoil-shaped elevator with a completely flat surface from which the two small front rudders were omitted. At a later date, small vertical areas were added at the outer limits of the fixed foreplane, being removed still later to their final position on the warp-wire struts beneath the main wings. Fabre also experimented with a small retractable keel surface underneath the front float; this was unsuccessful, but the siting of a similar structure behind each of the main floats did improve the directional control of the aircraft while hydroplaning. A series of six seaplanes is said to have been started after the May 1910 crash, but it is uncertain whether all were completed.

At Monaco in March 1911 the Fabre seaplane, in its latest form, made two flights in the hands of Jean Bécue; but on returning from the second of these, Bécue landed the machine too near to the shore, where it broke up in the surf. After this accident, Fabre had not the money to continue his flying experiments, but he concentrated on the design and manufacture of floats for other aircraft with considerable success during the period up to the outbreak of World War 1. In 1911 he designed floats for a Voisin canard biplane, which thus became the world's first amphibious aeroplane, and in the various events at the Monaco meeting in 1913, every winning machine was fitted with floats of Fabre design. The remains of the Fabre seaplane were eventually acquired and restored by the *Musée de l'Air* at Chalais-Meudon, where it is now on permanent display.

## Farman  12, 22, 23 & 25

The first aeronaut in the Farman family was Maurice (1877–1964), who became an adept balloonist in 1894 and was responsible for taking his elder brother Henry (1873–1958) into the air for the first time. Henry[*] later flew in the Lebaudy airship in 1904, and began to take up gliding three years later. On 1 June 1907 he began an outstanding career in the realm of powered flight by ordering a biplane from the Voisin brothers, with which he made the first flight on 20 September. This Voisin–Farman I, then called Henri Farman No. 1, was only the third powered Voisin to be built, and was fitted with a 50 h.p. Antoinette pusher engine. Its wing span was 33 ft. 5½ in. (10·20 m.) but at Far-

man's request did not have the wing side-curtains then customary on Voisin aircraft. He had other alterations made to it subsequently, reducing the span of the tail cellule, replacing the biplane forward elevator by a single surface, and giving the wings a small degree of dihedral. On 9 November 1907 he won the prize offered by Ernest Archdeacon for the first recorded flight of 150 m., qualifying easily with a distance of some 3,380 ft. (1,030 m.) and staying in the air for some 74 seconds – the first flight of more than a minute to be made by a non-Wright aeroplane. It was also, as it happened, the first 1 km. closed circuit flight made in Europe, but since it was not being observed officially as such Farman had to repeat the performance at Issy on 13 January 1908 to qualify for the Deutsch-Archdeacon prize of 50,000 frs. offered for this feat. Some of this money was then spent on renewing the aeroplane's fabric and in buying a 50 h.p. Renault engine with which, as the Voison-Farman I*bis*, it made its first flight on 14 March. Evidently the Renault was unsatisfactory, for the Antoinette was reinstalled. In May an inboard pair of side-curtains was added, and after a short summer visit to New York a second pair of curtains was fitted at the wing extremities. These improved the aircraft's stability, but it still had no means of lateral control, a factor which Farman remedied in October 1908 by fitting ailerons – the first really practical ones Europe had seen – to both top and bottom wings. On 29 September the I*bis*

---

[*] The son of British parents, domiciled in Paris, Henry Farman retained British nationality until 1937. For most of his life he spelt his Christian name in the English way, although he alternated between the English and French forms during his early years in aviation with apparent unconcern. On all his early aircraft, however, up to and including the Henri Farman No. 2, he utilised the French spelling.

had made its best flight yet, of 26 miles (42 km.), but so far had only flown at modest heights within the safe perimeter of an aerodrome. It was thus a considerable step forward when, on 30 October (still with the ailerons fitted), Farman made a 16·75 mile (27 km.) cross-country flight – the first in Europe – from Bouy to Rheims. On 31 October, he set a new national height record in the Ibis of 82 ft. (25 m.). These achievements were followed by the retrograde step of converting the Ibis into a rudimentary triplane by adding a second cellule, of about two-thirds the overall span, on top of the existing one and extending the span of the uppermost rear elevator. Performance suffered as a result, and Farman sold the machine early in 1909 to an Austrian buyer.

The title Henri Farman No. 2 – first given to a freakish but mercifully uncompleted project called the 'Flying Fish' about a year earlier – was now accorded to a new and improved Voisin biplane which Farman had commissioned, but the Voisin brothers brazenly sold the completed machine instead to Mr. J. T. C. Moore-Brabazon. By doing so, they inadvertently rendered an incalculable service both to Henry Farman and to the whole cause of European aviation, for Farman was so disgusted with their action that he cancelled his order and decided to set up his own factory.

He called the first product of this factory the Henry Farman III, and in its original form it still retained features of the Voisin type, including the cellular tail assembly and 50 h.p.

Vivinus engine, but its full set of ailerons made it a much more controllable and efficient design. The first flight was made at Châlons on 6 April 1909, and several successful test flights were made during the spring and summer. By the time of the Rheims air meeting in August, Farman had replaced the Voisin-type tail unit with an open biplane tail and twin trailing rudders, and during the meeting the aircraft was re-engined with a 50 h.p. Gnome. This vastly improved the aircraft's performance, to the extent that the Farman III carried off the prize for distance with an oustanding flight of 112 miles (180 km.), and won other prizes for its altitude and passenger-carrying performance. Another marked advance over contemporary European machines was the Farman III's wheel-and-skid landing gear; as *Flight* remarked after the meeting, 'The Farman seemed to come to earth most perfectly and with least shock, for none was softer even when he had two passengers aboard.' Two 'production' Farman III's also flew well at Rheims, and later that year the type was introduced to an English audience by Louis Paulhan.

For 1910 Henry Farman scaled up the Type III to a fuselage length of 43 ft. 3⅝ in. (13·20 m.), with wings 34 ft. 1½ in. (10·40 m.) in span and 538·2 sq. ft. (50 sq. m.) in area. This model could reach 40 m.p.h. (65 km/hr.) with a 50 h.p. Gnome engine and 47 m.p.h. (75 km/hr.) with a 60 h.p. E.N.V. installed. Extensions to the upper wings bore the only two ailerons now fitted.

From then on, Henry Farman biplanes went from strength to strength, becoming among the most reliable and widely-used aeroplanes of the pre-war period, not only in Europe but in many other parts of the world. In the dramatic London–Manchester race fought out between Grahame-White and Paulhan (*qqv.*) in 1910, both men flew Henry Farmans. Grahame-White in particular was an enthusiastic flier of Farman machines, and in his 'Wake up, England!' campaign in summer 1912 two of these aircraft were included in the 'circus' that toured the British countryside. They were powered by Gnome engines and had interchangeable wheel or float undercarriages. One of Grahame-White's favourite stunts was to fly at night with the Farman's outline illuminated by scores of electric light bulbs strung along the wings and fuselage.

Maurice Farman's successes were less spectacular than those of his brother, but none the less worthy. His first powered aircraft venture was the Farman–Kellner–Neubauer, a joint design intended to combine the better features of the Wright and Voisin biplanes. Its first flight was made at Buc on 1 February 1909, with a 60 h.p. Renault replacing the 40 h.p. E.N.V. originally fitted, but after travelling some 985 ft. (300 m.) it landed heavily and was damaged. With modifications that included the addition of side-curtains to wings and tail, it was reflown in the autumn and subsequently flew quite successfully. This machine, sometimes called the MF.1, was the progenitor of the MF.7 'Longhorn' that first appeared in 1912 and which is described in the *Fighters 1914–19* volume of this series. The MF.11 'Shorthorn' was a later but on the whole less effective design without the long front skids and forward elevator of the MF.7, but both types gave useful service in the years immediately before and after the outbreak of World War 1. Interim types in this line of development were flown by Maurice Tabuteau in capturing the 1910 distance record of 363·35 miles (584·745 km.); and by A. Fourny, who secured the 1912 record with 628·15 miles (1,017 km.). Another notable flight involving a Maurice Farman biplane was that from St. Cloud to Puy-de-Dôme by Eugène Renaux and Albert Senouque on 7 March 1911. This 227 mile (366 km.) journey finished at an altitude of 4,593 ft. (1,400 m.) above sea level and was probably the first in which full use was made of compass, maps and weather reports.

**Flanders** 44

Formerly an assistant of A. V. Roe, Howard Flanders began to build the first aeroplane of his own design, the F.1, in the autumn of 1910, but was forced to abandon it in May 1911 when the 120 h.p. A.B.C. Vee-type engine ordered for it failed to arrive. He started upon a new aircraft, the F.2, designed round a 60 h.p. Green inline, and completed and flew this at Brooklands early in August 1911. The F.2 was an elegant and well-constructed machine, with wings of 35 ft. 0 in. (10·67 m.) span and 200 sq. ft. (18·58 sq. m.) area. It was flown by several of the pilots at Brooklands, including R. C. Kemp, who also flew it in October when competing for the British Empire Michelin trophies. Further modifications produced the slightly faster F.3, which differed chiefly in having enlarged wings and (later) a small fixed fin; the F.3 was, in effect, a prototype for the military F.4 until written off in a crash on 13 May 1912.

For some reason the Flanders F.4, with the increased power provided by a 70 h.p. Renault and with slightly shorter wings of 40 ft. 6 in. (12·34 m.) span, was not entered for the Military Trials of 1912, despite the fact that four were on order for the War Office; but the Flanders' speed range, when put through their test programme in the summer, was better than that of any Trials competitor and exceeded only by the *hors concours* B.E.2. The F.4's were allocated Army serial numbers 265, 281, 422 and 439, but their career was soon curtailed by the October 1912 edict banning monoplanes from military service.

Flanders did have an entrant in the Military Trials, in the shape of the attractive B.2, a tractor biplane with lines reminiscent of the Roe Type E; but damage sustained on arrival at Larkhill prevented it from flying. Back at Brooklands, it made its first proper flight in December 1912 with a 40 h.p. A.B.C. (instead of the 100 h.p. A.B.C. intended) and carrying two passengers. A second engine change in October 1913, to a 60 h.p. Isaacson radial, increased its top speed appreciably, and a further change came in June 1914 when a 70 h.p. Gnome was installed. The B.2 was eventually taken on R.N.A.S. charge with the serial number 918 and based at Great Yarmouth during the early part of World War 1; but meanwhile, in the late autumn of 1913, the company had been declared bankrupt. In the summer of 1914 Howard Flanders joined the Aviation Department of Vickers Ltd., where he designed the F.B.7 (virtually a scaled-up B.2 with twin engines) and the F.B.11.

## Fokker 39

The interest of Anthony Herman Gerard Fokker, then an eighteen-year-old student, was awakened in 1908 by the visit to France of Wilbur Wright. The young Dutchman was obliged to wait until two years later, when he had completed his military service, before getting a chance to build an aeroplane of his own. Then, at the Automobil Fachschule at Zalbach, near Mainz in Germany, he teamed up with Franz von Daum, a fellow student and a former *Oberleutnant* in the German Army. Their first aeroplane, a monoplane, was financed jointly by the two men, possibly with some contribution from the school as well. von Daum, who was Fokker's senior by some thirty years, also contributed a 50 h.p. Argus engine to the partnership. Construction of the aeroplane was begun in the early autumn of 1910 in the school's workshop at Wiesbaden; some assistance may also have been given by the works of

Jacob Goedecker, a local builder of *Taube*-type monoplanes with whom Fokker was later associated. Testing of the machine probably began in November 1910, and a rudder was added after taxying trials revealed a lack of directional control. Lateral control was effected by warping the dihedral wings, which were soon given a modest degree of sweepback to improve stability, and the rear edges of the tailplane were similarly controlled to perform as an elevator. By December Fokker was able to make a hop-flight of about 100 m., but during his absence for the Christmas holidays von Daum (whom Fokker had – not without reason – so far prevented from flying the aeroplane) decided to try to take the machine up himself. Instead, he succeeded only in taxying the aircraft into a tree and making it a virtual write-off.

The opportunity was taken to construct a new machine from the wreckage (among which the Argus engine had survived), and this time Goedecker played a bigger part in the design as well as undertaking the construction. There were a number of major differences from the first machine, notably the use of ailerons in place of the former wing-warping method of lateral control and simplification of the undercarriage. Elevators and a conventional rudder were fitted, and more extensive use of steel tubing was made in the airframe. On this aeroplane, on 16 May 1911, Fokker passed the tests for his pilot's brevet – an event that reinforced von Daum's determination to learn to fly it, with the result that

again he crashed and again the machine was wrecked. After this Fokker ended their association by purchasing the German's share in the aircraft. With Goedecker, he then planned and built a third aircraft, again making use of the original Argus engine, which had survived the second crash. Completed in August 1911, it was appreciably smaller than its 42 ft. $7\frac{3}{4}$ in. (13·00 m.) span predecessor, and on Fokker's insistence the ailerons were omitted. It was capable of carrying a passenger, had a better performance than either of the first two machines, and even without a system of lateral control was basically stable in calm weather. (When taken back in August 1911 for demonstration in Fokker's homeland, it acquired the nickname *Haarlem Spin* (Haarlem Spider). Some sources refer to it as *Spin III*, giving the earlier Fokker-von Daum monoplanes the titles *Spin I* and *Spin II*; but, strictly, the third monoplane was the first 'Spider'.)

Early in 1912 the Fokker Aeroplanbau G.m.b.H. was formed at Johannisthal bei Berlin, and here some twenty-five *Spin*-type monoplanes were subsequently assembled from components built in the Goedecker workshops. The initial version was the A-1912 2-seater, in which the 50 h.p. Argus was the standard engine; later in the year versions appeared with a 60 or 70 h.p. Argus, and the B-1912 with a 100 h.p. unit. A few *Spins* had 70 h.p. Renault engines, one was fitted with a 95 h.p. Mercedes for military trials and another flown experimentally with a 50 h.p. Gnome rotary, but the majority of those built had Argus powerplants. They were employed both as privately-owned competitive aircraft and at the Fokker flying school at Schwerin, and were fitted with assorted seat fairings or fuselage shells offering varying degrees of protection for the occupants. Those tested by the Prussian Army were designated M.1. Production *Spins* had stick-type (instead of wheel-type) controls and the rearmost cabane pylon situated further aft, level with the tailplane leading edge.

In certain respects, Anthony Fokker might be compared to his Anglo-American contemporary S. F. Cody. Neither had any especial technical knowledge or inclination, but both were natural pilots of great skill and courage, with an instinctive sense of whether an aeroplane was 'right'; and in an age when much advance was still by trial and error, such a gift was often worth a dozen degrees in mechanical engineering. It certainly contributed to the pilot-appeal of the fighters which Fokker later produced for Germany, several of which are described in the *Fighters 1914–19* volume in this series.

## Goupy 61

The designs of Ambroise Goupy were not, of themselves, outstanding in terms of performance, but his 1909 biplanes at least deserve a place in the chronology of aeroplane development. They were preceded in 1908 by the Goupy I, a large tri-plane of the boxkite type, which

Goupy had had built at the Voisin factory at Billancourt. The wing and tail structures bore a superficial resemblance to those of the contemporary Voisin biplanes, but the Goupy I had a fabric-covered fuselage with a single cockpit, in front of which was installed a 50 h.p. Renault engine driving a disproportionately small tractor propeller. Wing span of the Goupy I was 24 ft. 7¼ in. (7·50 m.) and the aircraft weighed some 1,102 lb. (500 kg.). The conception of providing adequate lift in a sturdier and more compact form by using a triple-wing layout was not new – it had been propounded by Sir George Cayley in 1843 and by John Stringfellow in 1868 – but Goupy was among the first to complete a full-size, powered machine with this configuration. On 5 September 1908, some eight months before the hop-flights of A. V. Roe's *Bull's-eye* at Lea Marshes, the Goupy I made its first hop at Issy-les-Moulineaux, but it was not a notably successful machine. Only three further hops were made, the last being on 7 December and the longest covering only 492 ft. (150 m.), and after these Goupy abandoned this design.

Construction of his next machine, the Goupy II, was undertaken in the Blériot workshops at Buc, and similarities to Blériot's Type XI cross-Channel aircraft were evident in the design of the Goupy's fuselage, trailing rudder and castoring three-wheeled undercarriage. Assistance with the design is ascribed to Lieutenant Mario Calderara of the Italian Navy, a former pupil of the

Wrights. The Goupy II was a tractor biplane, with pronounced forward stagger of the wings and the two horizontal tail surfaces. In its original form the tips of the lower elevator were made to pivot fore and aft, while ahead of the lower mainplane were two small frontal elevators. The aircraft was powered by a 25 h.p. R.E.P. semi-radial engine, had a wing span of 19 ft. 8¼ in. (6·00 m.) and weighed 639 lb. (290 kg.). It made its first flight, covering 656 ft. (200 m.), at Buc on 9 March 1909, with Goupy at the controls; later that day a second flight, of half the distance, was made by Calderara.

No record has been traced of other flights until 14 December 1909, by which time the aeroplane had been much modified and was a far more practical design. Known in its new form as the Goupy III, it now had a 30 h.p. Anzani engine. Both of the horizontal tail surfaces now had pivoting extremities, between which their fixed inner sections were united by fixed vertical fins to form a central box; and this method of providing lateral control was extended by adding pivoting tips to the upper and lower wings in lieu of the frontal elevons. No outstanding achievements were claimed for the Goupy III, but several were built. The French pilot Ladougne, who flew a Goupy at air meetings at Doncaster, Burton and Rheims, formed a flying school at Juvisy using machines of this type; and this was well enough patronised to stand as a recommendation for the aircraft's safety and general handling

qualities. Performances by the Goupy and Breguet designs, especially the latter, possibly did as much to consolidate the merits of tractor biplanes as did the Blériot XI on behalf of tractor monoplanes.

**Grahame-White** 24 & 25

Few individuals did more than Claude Grahame-White (1879–1959) to foster a spirit of air-mindedness among the non-flying British public. His 'Wake up, England!' campaign, during the summer of 1912, described under the Farman entry, was only one of many efforts he made to arouse interest in flying, and he was one of the first to exploit the aeroplane as a means of commercial transportation. Grahame-White learned to fly in France early in 1910, and for a short time ran a flying school in that country. His school in England – opened at Brooklands and removed later to Hendon – was to become the busiest in Europe, holding regular weekly displays and races as well as providing tuition.

Grahame-White first came into nation-wide prominence in April 1910 in the £10,000 London–Manchester race sponsored by the *Daily Mail* newspaper. He lost the race to the only other competitor, the Frenchman Louis Paulhan, but the honours were divided equally, for Grahame-White's effort had included a spectacular night flight to regain lost ground, and was the first of its kind in England. Six months later, at Belmont Park on New York's Long Island, he won the Gordon Bennett Trophy in his Farman at an average speed of 61 m.p.h. (98 km/hr.). Early in 1911 he began to associate with Sir Hiram Maxim with a view to developing aircraft for military use, and at Hendon in May demonstrated 'bomb dropping' with sandbags suspended under the wings of a Farman. Support for the proposed Grahame-White, Blériot & Maxim Company failed to materialise, but Grahame-White later obtained financial backing from the Chairman of the Dunlop Tyre Company and took over the whole concern. Pilots of the company – though not Grahame-White himself – took part in September 1911 in the first aerial postal service in Britain, flown between Hendon and Windsor as part of the Coronation Year celebrations of King George V.

The first aircraft designed by Grahame-White, the 2-seat Baby, was evolved during his U.S. tour of 1910, and was essentially a smaller edition of the Henry Farman biplane of which he was a devotee. Built by the Burgess factory at Marblehead, Massachusetts, it had been successfully test flown at Hendon before appearing at the Olympia Show in March 1911. A fast and manoeuvrable aircraft for its day, the Baby had a 27 ft. 0 in. (8·23 m.) wing span, a length of 32 ft. 3 in. (9·83 m.) and was powered by a 50 h.p. Gnome engine mounted, pusher fashion, mid-way between the wings. Grahame-White took it on a subsequent visit to the United States, where at least one other example was built. The first British-built products of the Gra-

hame-White Aviation Co. were a 1911 monoplane and the Type XV of 1912, another Farman-derived biplane also powered by a 50 h.p. Gnome. The latter was an unspectacular but reliable design, developed over the years until it had tapered wing extensions, balanced ailerons, an enclosed nacelle and dual controls for the crew, and improved engine installations. One hundred and thirty-five were built as trainers for the R.F.C. and R.N.A.S., and remained in service during the early part of World War 1. In-flight trials were made at Bisley on 27 November 1913, by a Type XV in which a Lewis machine-gunner sat on a special platform below the pilot.

In January 1913 appeared the first design for the company by J. D. North, later the Chairman and Managing Director of Boulton and Paul Ltd. Called the Popular, it was intended as a cheap (less than £400), easy-to-fly aircraft for flying schools or private customers of relatively modest means. The Popular was a 2-seat pusher biplane with unequal-span wings of 28 ft. 0 in. (8·53 m.) span, with a 4-hour endurance and a top speed of 50 m.p.h. (80 km/hr.) on the power of a 35 h.p. Anzani engine. It was a notable absentee from the Aero Show the following month, but two of North's other designs attracted much comment. One was a handsome 'sporting' 2-seater with a 60 h.p. Anzani engine and twin floats of ingenious design. These, according to Dallas Brett, were 'each provided with two little airscoops which collected the air as the machine rushed forward and forced it down channels through the float so that it emerged underneath just abaft the step and broke up the water's adhesion to the under skin of the float'. The other Olympia exhibit was the freakish Type VI, a Barber-inspired 'gunbus' which was North's competitor to the F.E.2 and the Vickers Destroyer. This was a nacelle-and-tailboom pusher biplane in which the nacelle encompassed three occupants – a pilot, an observer and a gunner armed with a Colt machine-gun – and a 90 h.p. Austro-Daimler engine at the front. The three tubular steel tailbooms formed a triangular section, and the tail control wires were led through the uppermost boom, which also acted as a propeller bearing. A later and less bizarre 'gunbus' was designed with a 50 h.p. Gnome engine and slightly sweptback wings.

In August 1913 the Charabanc (sometimes called the Aerobus) made its maiden flight. This represented the first real step towards realising Grahame-White's dream of a merchant air fleet, and was designed to carry a pilot and 4 passengers. It was extremely stable, and its load-carrying ability was convincingly demonstrated by Louis Noel on 2 October 1913, when he made a 19·75 min. flight with 9 passengers aboard. A month later a Charabanc, flown by Reginald Carr and fitted with a 100 h.p. Green engine (to qualify as an all-British machine), flew over a Brooklands–Hendon course for a total of 315 miles (507 km.) to win the British Empire Michelin Cup No. 1.

Grahame-White himself attempted a London–Paris flight in a Charabanc, but was forced to abandon the journey at Folkestone due to a fuel leak.

A contemporary of the Charabanc was the 'Lizzie' (also known as the 'Tea Tray'), a distinctive little machine whose body had obvious Morane overtones and whose wings came from one of the Popular biplanes. It gave many exhibitions at Hendon in 1913–14, latterly with the short lower wings much extended.

The last design by North before the outbreak of war was the Type XIII. Intended as a competitor for the 1914 Circuit of Britain, it was a 2-seat tractor biplane, powered by a 100 h.p. Gnome Monosoupape rotary engine, and originally mounted on a close-set pair of floats. The 27 ft. 3 in. (8·31 m.) fuselage was basically that of a Morane-Saulnier Type G, which the Grahame-White Co. was building under licence as its Type XIV, and the heavily staggered wings had a span of 27 ft. 10 in. (8·48 m.). Excellent manoeuvrability and a maximum speed of 85 m.p.h. (137 km/hr.) were claimed for the Type XIII, but the float arrangement was unsatisfactory and was replaced by a wheeled undercarriage.

## Handley Page 41

A determined individualist, Frederick Handley Page (1885–1962) followed a natural boyhood interest in making model aeroplanes by joining the Aeronautical Society in 1907 and becoming chairman of its exhibition committee the year after. Already a trained electrical engineer, his first acquaintance with aeroplane construction was a tandem-wing machine built for G. P. Deverall Saul. He took a stand at the March 1909 Olympia Aero Show, on which were exhibited a glider model and a full-size monoplane designed by José Weiss, and in June 1909 formed his own manufacturing company.

The first aeroplane of Handley Page's own devising was a crescent-winged single-seat monoplane with a cruciform rudder-cum-elevator similar to the kind used by Santos-Dumont. The shape of the 32 ft. 6 in. (9·91 m.) wings, and the greyish-blue colour of the rubberised fabric that covered them, led to the aircraft being known as the Bluebird, although it is often referred to also as the Handley Page Type A. With its original 25 h.p. Advance 4-cylinder engine the Bluebird refused to fly when tested at Creekmouth, near Barking. When this unsatisfactory unit was replaced by a 20–25 h.p. Alvaston 2-cylinder engine the aircraft rose and made a short hop, but was damaged as it landed. Handley Page rebuilt it into the Type C with a 65 h.p. Isaacson radial engine, and displayed it partially completed at Olympia in 1910; in May the aircraft made its first really successful take-off at Creekmouth.

A foretaste of future success was given by the Handley Page Type D, which earned much admiration at the March 1911 Aero Show for the beautiful finish of its varnished, mahogany-skinned fuselage. The Type D retained the Weiss-style crescent wings, but was fitted with more conventional separate tail control surfaces. It made a number of short hops with the original 35 h.p. Green engine, but after being refitted with a 60 h.p. Isaacson for the July 1911 Circuit of Britain was wrecked beyond repair before the date of the race arrived. But the Handley Page Type E, which appeared later in 1911 and was basically an improved and enlarged development of the D, was much more successful in terms of design. Whereas the Type D had been a single-seater, the E was a 2-seat machine, was powered by a 50 h.p. Gnome rotary engine, and had a long, shallow fixed fin. The fuselage was covered in thin mahogany ply sheet given several coats of copal varnish. The wing and tail surfaces were given a protective coating of cellulose whose bilious yellowish-green colour led to the Type E being nicknamed 'Antiseptic' or 'Yellow Peril'. Lieutenant Wilfred Parke was one of several well-known pilots to fly the Handley Page E with success; one notable effort was a 30 mile (48 km.) cross-country flight from Fairlop, Essex, to Brooklands in 1912. Parke, who in the twenty months of his flying career flew twenty-nine different types of aircraft, considered that the Type E 'for pure pleasure of flying is miles ahead of anything else I have been in'. The success of the Type E, which led Handley Page to acquire the Cricklewood premises that the company still occupies today, received a setback in 1912 when the aircraft suffered severe damage in a crash. However, it was rebuilt, with successive modifications that included a triangular vertical fin, a communal cockpit instead of the original separate ones, ailerons in place of wing-warping, a pyramid cabane pylon and a B.E.2-type undercarriage with twin skids inboard of the main wheels. When exhibited at Olympia in February 1913, it had flown more than 2,000 miles (3,219 km.) and carried over 100 passengers during the preceding 15 months.

The Handley Page Type F had a far shorter and less auspicious career. Built for the 1912 Military Trials, it was a single-seat, 43 ft. 6 in. (13·26 m.) span monoplane with a 70 h.p. Gnome engine. Flown by H. A. Petre, it made one flight in frightful weather conditions but on the second the wing was damaged when it had to land because of engine trouble. It was reflown in November with new wings of a modified shape, but on 15 December, while being flown by Lieutenant Parke, this highly experienced pilot inexplicably committed the elementary mistake of trying to turn the aircraft downwind with a faltering engine. Inevitably, the Gnome stalled and the machine dived into the ground, killing both occupants.

Two other pre-war Handley Page aircraft deserve mention. The Type G was a 2/3-seater with a 100 h.p. Anzani engine. Announced originally as a seaplane, it was built with a land undercarriage and had the fuselage suspended mid-way between the warp-controlled wings. It flew for the first time in November 1913 and was later tested at the Royal Aircraft Factory, recording a 70 m.p.h. (112·6 km./hr.) top speed and 300 ft/min. (1·52 m/sec.) initial climb while carrying two passengers. Sold later to the Northern Aircraft Company, it was chartered early in 1914 by Princess Ludwig von Lowenstein-Wertheim for a London–Paris flight, and by the summer had flown over 10,000 miles (16,093 km.) and carried 200 passengers. Later it was taken over by the R.N.A.S., who gave it the serial number 892 and continued to use it until 1915 as a military trainer. An enlarged development, the L/200, was begun in 1914 as a contender for the *Daily Mail*'s £10,000 prize offered for a trans-Atlantic flight. Spanning 60 ft. 0 in. (18·29 m.), it had an enclosed cabin with two side-by-side seats and was powered by a 200 h.p. Salmson (Canton-Unné) radial engine; but it had not been completed when war caused the competition to be cancelled.

**Hanriot** 45
René Hanriot, already well known in France as a Darracq racing car driver, designed his first aeroplane in 1907 and displayed it at the *Salon de l'Aéronautique* in October 1909. It was a frail looking but well constructed single-seat monoplane, with an open-framework fuselage, square-cut wings of some 31 ft. 2 in. (9·50 m.) span and powered by a

50 h.p. Buchet engine. In spring 1910 Hanriot opened a flying school at Béthény, not far from his Rheims workshop, where production of later monoplane designs was already under way. These included the 20 h.p. Darracq-engined *Libellule* (Dragonfly) and a somewhat larger machine with a 40 h.p. Gyp engine. New design features, before being introduced on a full-size machine, were executed in miniature and tested on a scale model powered by a 3 h.p. Dutheil-Chalmers engine. Among those assisting Hanriot were his son Marcel and another former Darracq racing driver, Louis Wagner. When awarded his pilot's brevet (No. 95) on 10 June 1910, the 15-year-old Marcel was the world's youngest flier.

A developed version of the Gyp-engined monoplane made its British debut in July 1910. At Lanark Marcel Hanriot flew an E.N.V.-engined model, while at Bournemouth one with a 40 h.p. Clerget was flown by Wagner. The Hanriot monoplanes were simple but elegant, lightly but strongly built, their most striking feature being the mahogany-skinned fuselage. Other monoplanes had appeared with bodies that looked like racing skiffs, but the Hanriot's was actually built like one, giving a sturdy frame that needed a minimum of wire bracing. A Hanriot 2-seater was entered, unsuccessfully, in the French *Concours Militaire* in late autumn 1911, but the era of the skiff-like monoplanes was almost over. Shortly after the French trials, Hanriot engaged the services of Monsieur Pagny, the

Nieuport chief designer, and his subsequent monoplanes had the same 'deep-chested' appearance as the contemporary Nieuports. A pair of Pagny-designed 2-seaters, each with a 100 h.p. Gnome, were entered for the British Military Trials in August 1912. Flown by S. V. Sippe and the Peruvian J. Bielovucic, they put up the best speed and climbing performance, showed good range potential, and by any rational system of judging Bielovucic's machine would have been a clear winner of the competition. As it was, Hanriot had to be content with only a small consolation prize. Attempts to promote the monoplanes commercially in Britain also met with disappointing results, and this lack of enthusiasm may have influenced Hanriot *père* in deciding to withdraw from aviation in 1913. (He was, however, to return to it soon after the outbreak of war, associating with Dupont in the excellent little HD-1 fighter.)

Backing for Pagny's designs was maintained by A. Ponnier, resulting in an excellent racing monoplane produced to compete for the 1913 Gordon Bennett Trophy. Like its great rival, the Deperdussin racer, the Ponnier monoplane had a 160 h.p. two-row Gnome engine; its wing span was 23 ft. 5½ in. (7·15 m.). Emile Védrines put up a fine performance over the course to finish a very close second to Prévost's Deperdussin. Later in 1913, Ponnier produced a number of biplane designs in the hope of military orders, but such rewards did not come until after the outbreak of war.

## McCurdy 15

The Aerial Experiment Association, financed and founded in September 1907 by Doctor and Mrs. Alexander Graham Bell, included among its members the Americans Glenn Curtiss (q.v.) and Lieutenant T. E. Selfridge, and two Canadians, F. W. ('Casey') Baldwin and John A. D. McCurdy. During its brief existence the A.E.A. was responsible for four aeroplanes; each was attributed to a different member of the team, although it is more likely that each was a joint endeavour. They were lineal descendants of the Wright gliders, based on data provided by the Wrights to Selfridge. All four were powered by Curtiss engines and were pusher biplanes whose upper and lower wingtips converged towards one another in bow-shaped curves.

First to fly, in March 1908, was Red Wing, attributed to Selfridge and flown by Baldwin at Hammondsport on the shore of Lake Keuka, near New York. It had no lateral control, and made only two hop-flights before crash-landing. In May 1908 various A.E.A. members flew the second machine, White Wing, including Baldwin, who was said to have been its designer. The European influence of Esnault-Pelterie and Blériot was apparent in the fitting of ailerons to White Wing – the first appearance of such a feature in a non-European aeroplane – and this aircraft also had a wheel undercarriage. But it, too, was short-lived, and like Red Wing was abandoned after a crash. The A.E.A.'s third machine was the June Bug, described under the Curtiss entry on page 116, and its fourth and last was the Silver Dart.

As originally projected in July 1908, the Silver Dart was similar to the June Bug, but larger and with a more powerful Curtiss engine between the upper and lower mainplanes with a chain-belt drive to two pusher propellers outboard of the rear fuselage framework. It had a tall single rudder and a single-plane front elevator. The design was finalised in mid-October with the engine now mounted on the lower wings, the rear fuselage booms lengthened and sited outboard of the propellers, the rudder height reduced and a biplane front elevator fitted. Like its predecessors, it was built at Hammondsport, but it was taken to ice-covered Baddeck Bay in Nova Scotia for its first flight. Additional pre-flight modifications included resiting the radiator further forward and on the centre-line; shortening the rear booms by about 1 ft. (0·30 m.); and shortening the main undercarriage legs, thereby decreasing the wings' angle of incidence. On 23 February 1909 the Silver Dart made a maiden flight of half a mile (0·80 km.) with McCurdy at the controls. Baldwin was the first Canadian pilot to fly, but at Baddeck Bay McCurdy became both the first man to fly in Canada and the first British Commonwealth subject to fly in a Commonwealth country. On the following day the Silver Dart made a 4½ mile (7·24 km.) flight, and within a few weeks had flown at least one trip of 12 miles (19·31 km.).

The Silver Dart contributed nothing new to the world's store of aeronautical knowledge, and after its completion the A.E.A. was disbanded. McCurdy continued to fly it, and altogether it completed some 200 or more flights, though they served little purpose beyond making him a more experienced pilot. However, it consolidated his interest in aviation, and later in 1909 he formed the Canadian Aerodrome Company (the A.E.A. had, for some reason, always used Langley's term 'aerodrome' in preference to 'aeroplane'). Two military biplanes, the Baddeck 1 and 2, were built by this organisation on similar lines to the A.E.A. aircraft, and the Baddeck 1 was demonstrated before members of the Canadian Militia Council in August 1909, but both aircraft eventually crashed and the company went into liquidation. In August 1910, back in the New York area, McCurdy was concerned in some of the very first ground-to-air radio telegraphy experiments; later, he became manager of the Canadian branch of the Curtiss Company at Toronto, where production of the JN-3 was undertaken for Britain during the war years.

## Martin and Handasyde 43

The partnership formed in 1908 between H. P. Martin and G. H. Handasyde produced some of the most handsome and workmanlike aeroplanes built by the embryo British aircraft industry before World War 1. They were clearly inspired by the earlier Antoinette (q.v.) monoplanes, but Handasyde,

a born designer, introduced several original improvements. The partners' first machine had to be repaired after its 22 h.p. Beeston engine shook loose from its bearers during the first run-up, but it was subsequently tested at Barking. Further damage, sustained during its transfer to Halifax, was repaired on arrival, but when high winds blew down its tent hangar the machine was completely wrecked. A second, larger machine appeared in the spring of 1910. During a career of some four and a half years this aeroplane underwent a series of modifications. The original Beeston engine was replaced by a 35 h.p. J.A.P., and conventional controls were installed in place of the Antoinette type previously fitted. In this form the aircraft bore the legend 'No. 3 Martin-Handasyde'. In the summer of 1911 a 35 h.p. Green engine was substituted, but the J.A.P. was later reinstalled. The aircraft was still in existence in August 1914.

Martin and Handasyde's next machine, a 2-seater, was the Type 4B (or B4) Dragonfly, built for Mr. T. O. M. Sopwith and displayed at the 1911 Aero Show at Olympia. It was originally powered by a 50 h.p. Gnome engine and had a span of 37 ft. 0 in. (11·28 m.). The slender, skiff-like fuselage was completed by a conventional tail assembly, but the warp-controlled wings, although generally similar to the Antoinette in planform, had a deeper camber than those of the French archetype. The 'Martinsyde' monoplanes of the period were appreciably faster than most of their contemporaries, and were very responsive to their controls. At a later stage, the Dragonfly was refitted with a 65 h.p. Antoinette engine.

In the late autumn of 1911 another 2-seater appeared, which from the start had a 65 h.p. Antoinette in a well-contoured metal cowling. This machine, sometimes called 'the magnificent Martinsyde', was flown extensively at Brooklands by Sopwith, Gordon Bell and Graham Gilmour from November 1911; but on 17 February 1912, while flying in very turbulent weather, it broke up in the air and Gilmour was killed.

Martin and Handasyde's first military monoplane, which appeared in summer 1912, strengthened its resemblance to the Antoinette by having a similar bank of tubular condensers on each side of the forward fuselage, although the new, rigidly constructed tail surfaces struck an individualistic note. Two were delivered to the War Office during 1912, but the monoplane ban of that autumn ended their military career before it had begun and they do not appear in the initial listing of Army serial numbers. A developed version was evolved for the 1912 Military Trials, but trouble was experienced with its 90 h.p. Chenu engine and the aircraft spent most of its time on the ground with a faulty magneto. After the Trials it was fitted with a 65 h.p. Antoinette.

The Martinsyde monoplane shown at Olympia in February 1913, which had started its career with an 80 h.p. Laviator (Dansette-Gillet) engine, was subsequently given a 120 h.p. Austro-Daimler, with which it put up some excellent performances before being wrecked by Gordon Bell on 13 June 1913. Another basically similar machine was then nearing completion, also with an Austro-Daimler engine, and this made its first flight in September. Later that month, flown by R. H. Barnwell, it gained second place in the second Aerial Derby, and on a subsequent test at the Royal Aircraft Factory recorded a speed of 97 m.p.h. (156 km/hr.). In February 1914 there appeared a third and even more handsome Austro-Daimler Martinsyde, which was still at Shoreham when war broke out six months later.

The most promising pre-war Martin-Handasyde was the big monoplane designed to be flown by Gustav Hamel in an attempt for the *Daily Mail*'s prize of £10,000 for the first transatlantic crossing. With a 215 h.p. Sunbeam engine, wing span of 65 ft. 0 in. (19·81 m.) and gross weight of 4,800 lb. (2,177 kg.), it was in essence a scaled-up version of the earlier 2-seaters, though the 770 sq. ft. (71·54 sq. m.) straight-tapered wings had raked-back tips and were still warp-controlled. Special features included a telescopic signalling mast and a 14 ft. (4·27 m.) watertight compartment in the fuselage. The big Martinsyde, one of the most powerful aircraft of its day, might have had a good chance of success, and was nearing completion when, on 23 May 1914, Hamel was lost in a flight over the

Channel. Work continued in the hope that a sponsor and/or a new pilot would be forthcoming, but the venture finally had to be abandoned upon the outbreak of war.

The company also began, for the 1914 Aerial Derby, an Antoinette-engined pusher biplane. This departed from the technique used in earlier machines by making extensive use of steel tube for the airframe, but it was not completed in time for the race. The company's next products, including the wartime S.1 scout, and the F.4 Buzzard and G.100 and G.102 'Elephant' fighters, were all biplanes.

## Morane-Saulnier  56

In the two or three years preceding the outbreak of World War 1 the monoplanes produced by the Morane-Saulnier partnership were widely regarded as among the best of their kind, and many notable performances were recorded by them and their pilots. The Type A, flown in October 1911, was the first product to emanate from the brothers Léon and Robert Morane in their new association with Raymond Saulnier. (Previously, in addition to their own flying activities, they had been connected with certain of the Borel designs.) The Type A was a single-seat, warp-controlled, shoulder-wing monoplane with a 50 h.p. Gnome rotary. About a dozen were built for the *Aviation Militaire*, by whom they were designated MS.11. Exports variants with 80 h.p. Gnomes were the Type C (five for Russia), and the Type F (two for Rumania).

Another 1911 design was the Type PP, so called because of the 440-mile (708-km.) flight made in it from Pau to Paris by Maurice Tabuteau.

The definitive pre-war Moranes were the Types G and H of 1912. These were a notable improvement over the earlier monoplanes, usually having fully-enclosed fuselages and 80 h.p. Gnome engines. The Type G was a 2-seater and the Type H a single-seater, but they were otherwise fundamentally alike. Ninety-four Type G's and twenty-six Type H's were built for the *Aviation Militaire*, the former batch including a proportion of floatplanes designated GA (60 h.p. Le Rhône) and GB (80 h.p. Gnome) with increased span. Among the early feats accomplished in Morane-Saulnier monoplanes was the altitude record of 18,405 ft. (5,610 m.) at Tunis in 1912 by Roland Garros. The following year brought many new triumphs for the Moranes. Gustav Hamel, in a Type H converted to a racing single-seater with the wings cropped to 20 ft. (6·10 m.), won the U.K. Aerial Derby at 76 m.p.h. (122 km/hr.); later, in a specially strengthened machine, he became the second man in Britain to perform the loop. Between 10 June and 2 July 1913, M. Brindejonc des Moulinais made a much-acclaimed tour of Europe in his Morane, covering some 3,107 miles (5,000 km.). Garros, in a Morane-Saulnier monoplane with only a 60 h.p. engine, became the first man to cross the Mediterranean by air, making the 460-mile (740-km.)

crossing from St. Raphaël to Bizerta on 23 September. Some three weeks later, on 16 October, a Morane figured in the first official postal flight in France when Lieutenant Ronin of the *Aviation Militaire* flew a consignment of mail from Villacoublay to Pauillac, near Bordeaux. Early in 1914 another notable endurance flight was completed by Marc Pourpe, who made a 2,734 mile (4,400 km.) round trip from Cairo to Khartoum and back between 4 January and 3 February. Another modified Morane won the 1914 U.K. Aerial Derby, flown by W. L. Brock, who later won other races (London–Manchester and Hendon–Paris) in the same aircraft.

Other pre-war monoplanes included the 1912 Type M, an experimental military aircraft with an armoured front fuselage; the 1913 Type I (or MS.6) scout for the *Aviation Militaire* (thirty-eight built); and the 2-seat Type BI ordered by the Russian Navy. The Type T, the first twin-engined venture (two 80 h.p. Le Rhône rotaries), was a 3-seat reconnaissance biplane not put into production until 1916, but its first flight was made in July 1914. Other famous wartime Moranes first flown in 1913 included the Types L and LA parasol-winged scouts and the Type N monoplane fighter; these are described in the *Fighters 1914–19* volume.

**Nieuport** 54 & 55
The Société Anonyme des Etablissements Nieuport, celebrated during and after World War 1 for its

excellent range of biplane fighters, was formed at Issy-les-Moulineaux in 1909 by the engineer-sportsman Edouard de Niéport (1875–1911). The company's pre-war products were all monoplanes, the first notable one making its public appearance in the summer of 1910 to the accompaniment of much favourable comment. The pilot was completely encompassed, except for his head, by the fully covered 27 ft. 6¾ in. (8·40 m.) fuselage, and entered his cockpit by a small door beneath the port wing. The wings themselves had a 32 ft. 9¾ in. (10·00 m.) span, and were warp-controlled by a rocker shaft operated by foot pedals. A semi-circular tailplane was fixed on top of the rear fuselage, behind which was a one-piece elevator bearing twin rudders. Flown by Edouard de Niéport at Rheims in July 1910, the little Nieuport was rated by many observers as the best competing aircraft, and it reached some 45 m.p.h. (72 km/hr.) on the modest 20 h.p. of its Darracq engine. At Olympia in March 1911 Nieuport exhibited a developed version of this monoplane, the Type IIN, powered by a 28 h.p. Nieuport engine, and at Mourmelon on 11 May an aircraft of this type was flown at a new world record speed of 74·37 m.p.h. (119·68 km/hr.).

There also appeared in 1911 a 2-seat Nieuport monoplane, the Type IVG, powered by a 50 h.p. Gnome and having a more orthodox tail assembly including a quadrant-shaped rudder. This was ordered by the Italian Army air corps, and was in service in North Africa before the end of the year. In one, on 24 October 1911, Capitano Moizo made the second-ever reconnaissance flight by a military aeroplane. At the *Concours Militaire* in October/November the Nieuport was brilliantly flown by the American pilot C. T. Weymann to emerge the winner of the contest. Ten monoplanes were ordered by the French Army, which also purchased the original *Concours* machine. Four or five Nieuports were on R.F.C. charge in mid-1912, and at least a dozen float-fitted Nieuports were used for training by the R.N.A.S. (Of incidental interest, the 'B.4' identification carried by the Nieuport illustrated on page 70 was the first form of military serial to be exhibited on British aircraft other than those built by the Army Aircraft Factory.) In the civil field also, 1911 was a successful year for the Nieuport monoplane. At Châlons, Edouard de Niéport captured a speed record of 82·73 m.p.h. (133·14 km/hr.), while at Buc, Gobé set up a new closed circuit distance record of 459·968 miles (740·255 km.). Weymann's Nieuport was unplaced in the June Circuit of Europe, but at Eastchurch in July, in the race for the Gordon Bennett Trophy, the French monoplanes were well represented. Edouard de Niéport, in a 70 h.p. Gnome-engined machine, finished third with a course average of 75·07 m.p.h. (120·74 km/hr.); and the race winner was Weymann in a 100 h.p. Gnome version with a speed of 78 m.p.h. (125·53 km/hr.).

After the death of Edouard de Niéport in a flying accident on 15 September 1911, the work of the company was continued by his brother Charles until he too died in a crash-landing on 24 January 1913. The Nieuport monoplanes, however, continued to be built and sold to a variety of customers and to be involved in events of significance. In 1913 these included a round trip over the Mediterranean from St. Raphaël to Ajaccio in Corsica and back again, by Lieutenants Destrem and de l'Escaille of the *Marine Nationale*; a world altitude record of 20,079 ft. (6,120 m.) by Georges Legagneux, also at St. Raphaël, in a Le Rhône-engined Nieuport; and an outstanding seven-week journey from Villacoublay to Cairo at the end of the year by Marc Bonnier and a passenger in an 80 h.p. Gnome-engined Nieuport. On the military side, Nieuport monoplanes were used in some of the very first static and airborne tests with a machine-gun fitted to an aeroplane, although the gun was mounted on a tubular 'pulpit' on top of the fuselage to fire above the sweep of the propeller. On 20 August 1913, Lieutenant Nesterov of the Imperial Russian Air Service became the first man ever to perform a successful loop, in a Nieuport. The Nieuport VIG (80 h.p. Gnome) was a military 2-seater used in some numbers pre-war in France, Italy (where it was built under licence by Macchi and others) and Russia, and a monoplane with a fully armoured fuselage was also built in 1913. The change to sesquiplanes, characteristic of the wartime Nieuport scouts, began with the Type 10, the first Nieuport evolved by the talented Gustave Delage, who joined the company in January 1914.

## Paulhan 18

Although he achieved greater prominence as a pilot than as a designer and builder of aeroplanes, Louis Paulhan (1883–1963) was associated with the production of at least two novel types of aircraft during his early career. Having taken part in building the airship *Ville de Paris* in 1907, Paulhan in the following year won a model aeroplane competition held by the *Aéro Club de France*; his prize was a Voisin biplane. It did not have an engine, but early in 1909 Paulhan was lucky enough to get one of the first Gnome rotary engines, which he installed in his biplane. He quickly became an excellent pilot, appearing with success at meetings in France, England and the United States. Paulhan came into widespread prominence on 27–28 April 1910 when, flying a Henry Farman biplane, he won a dramatic race against England's Claude Grahame-White (*q.v.*) from London to Manchester for the £10,000 prize put up by the *Daily Mail* newspaper. Earlier that month he had taken some of the first photographs from an aeroplane in France, and a little later was involved in similar activities in New York.

In later times Paulhan was much associated with water-borne aircraft, an interest that derived from an early association with Henri Fabre (*q.v.*), builder of the first European seaplane. Fabre allowed Paulhan to adopt his unique mono-spar wing construction in an aircraft of Paulhan's own design, which made its public debut at the Paris *Salon* in October 1910. Unlike Fabre's seaplane, however, this was both a landplane and a biplane, with a twin-girder 'fuselage' on which was lightly attached an aluminium nacelle encompassing side-by-side seats for pilot and passenger, with fuel tank, engine and 2-blade pusher propeller to the rear. The rigid construction of the wings needed no tie-wires, the sole bracing consisting of two I-type interplane struts on each side. As with the Fabre machine, the fabric was formed into pockets, slipped over each cantilevered rib and held taut to each rib end by a spring clip; thus it could be partially or completely rolled up to vary the wing area or during storage. The forward elevator, rudder and horizontal tail areas were similarly treated. Another novel feature was the use of leather hinges and fittings instead of the more usual metal type. Describing the aircraft in its issue of 26 October 1910, *The Aero* remarked 'it hardly bears any resemblance to one's hitherto conceived ideas of a flying machine', but conceded that 'if it does not perform well in future it will not be for lack of thought and experience on the part of its designers and its pilot'. Through the agency of Mr. G. Holt Thomas the British War Office purchased an aircraft of this kind; it was delivered before the formation of the Air Battalion, Royal Engineers, in

March 1911, but its ultimate fate is uncertain. The type continued to fly for a time in France, but was not generally adopted.

Paulhan was also associated in 1911 with the veteran designer Victor Tatin in building the latter's *Aéro-Torpille* (aerial torpedo). This single-seat monoplane had turned-up wingtips and a remarkably well streamlined wooden monocoque fuselage that did indeed resemble a torpedo in shape. Its 50 h.p. Gnome engine was completely concealed within the centre of the fuselage, driving a pusher propeller behind the tail by means of an extension shaft. It flew sufficiently well during 1911–12 for Tatin to describe it as a *'bon projectile'*, but its efficiency was not as outstanding as its appearance suggested and it was eventually abandoned.

## Phillips 79

The name of Horatio Frederick Phillips (1845–1926) should appear high on the list of early pioneers who made important contributions to aeronautical progress, for he established the foundation upon which all modern aerofoils have been based. This stemmed from earlier experiments with hydrofoils, and was based on the supposition that a differentially cambered structure, with a more pronounced curve on the upper surface than on the lower, induces extra lift by decreasing the pressure along its top. In the two final decades of the last century he took out a variety of patents; the most important were those in 1884 for 'wings with slightly thick-ened leading edge, so curved on the top surface that a vacuum is produced', and in 1891 for 'wing sections of increased lift, made of sufficient depth to contain spars, and having a bulged nose portion with flattened entry on the underside'. Informative accounts of Phillips' various projects are scarce, and I am indebted for much of the following material to an article appearing in *The Aero* of 18 January 1910.

A man of diverse talents, Phillips also designed his own engines, and while still in his early twenties attempted a vertical take-off machine with a steam engine driving two co-axial, counter-rotating propellers. When tested at Battersea, however, it could not lift its own weight from the ground. Phillips then experimented for a time at Norwood with unpowered control-line models of boxkite pattern launched by catapult to glide around a circular track. Later experiments with full-size machines of similar design were eventually abandoned, Phillips apparently considering their fabric-covered side surfaces more of a hindrance than a help in windy weather, and he began instead the studies leading to the 'Phillips entry' aerofoil patents of 1884 and 1891. To arrive at an ideal sectional form he built a steam-driven 'whirling table' device – analogous to the more modern centrifuge – allied to a steam-injected wind tunnel.

The first application of the Phillips entry principle in a full-scale device seems to have been the machine which underwent tethered tests around a 200 ft. (61 m.) diameter wooden track at Harrow in 1893. Weighing 416 lb. (188·7 kg.) including a deadweight load of 56 lb. (25·4 kg.), it was powered by a steam engine of about 6 h.p. with a chain and bevel drive to a pusher propeller with two paddle-shaped blades. The 3-wheeled chassis was in the form of an elongated triangle, and the lifting surface consisted of a rectangular frame with ten upright supporting members and fifty of Phillips' aerofoil 'sustainers' mounted horizontally, making the complete unit resemble a a giant Venetian blind. The sustainers had an approximate span of 19 ft. (5·80 m.) and a chord of about $1\frac{1}{2}$ in. (3·81 cm.) each. Although not meant to fly, his multiplane generated considerable lift and is reputed to have travelled through the air for some 150–250 ft. (46–76 m.).

*The Aero* reports that Phillips made several subsequent full-size aeroplanes including at least three VTOL projects. The first two, driven by petrol engines, were tested *circa* 1900 and 1902 at Crystal Palace, but were complete failures. The third, tested in autumn 1909, 'gave promising results, and is to be followed by another which he hopes will be ready for trial during the coming summer'. Reference is also made to a machine with inclined rotors, intended to run along the ground before rising, which may have been a modified form of the second Crystal Palace machine. It was apparently tested at

Mitcham, but with what result is not stated. In 1904 appeared the first man-carrying multiplane (Phillips I). This had a framework of twenty rigid blade sustainers, of a more substantial section than those previously used, and was driven by a 22 h.p. piston engine (presumably designed by Phillips) with a wooden 2-blade tractor propeller. It weighed, with the pilot aboard, about 600 lb. (272 kg.). Lifting qualities were as good as those of the 1893 tethered rig, but the multiplane lacked longitudinal stability and control; consequently it suffered several mishaps and underwent a number of design changes, particularly to the undercarriage and tail control surfaces. The configuration illustrated is a typical one, though it cannot be dated with any certainty. The 1904 multiplane had an 'unstick' speed of some 34 m.p.h. (55 km/hr.), and was tested at Streatham, but apparently made no flights of significant length.

A little more is known about the 1907 multiplane, sometimes called the Phillips II. It had a similar powerplant to the Phillips I but marked a return to the 50-slat frame of very narrow sustainers. This time, however, there were four such frames, mounted on a quadricycle undercarriage with the pilot seated between the middle two frames. The engine, which drove a 7 ft. (2·13 m.) wooden tractor propeller, was mounted at the front, and the machine weighed about 500 lb. (227 kg.) without its pilot. It was 15 ft. (4·57 m.) long, had a span of 20 ft. (6·10 m.) and stood 10 ft. (3·05 m.) high. Tested at Streatham in spring-summer 1907, the Phillips II made a number of hop-flights, including a very creditable one of about 510 ft. (155 m.) that entitles it to be regarded as the first powered aircraft to fly in England, albeit for a relatively short distance. Its fore and aft stability was considerably better than any of Phillips' earlier machines.

Evidence exists of at least one other man-carrying multiplane. This reverted to a single 'Venetian blind' made up of one hundred and ten narrow slats, was mounted on a cumbersome undercarriage with two heavy wooden skids inboard of the main wheels, and had no tail control surfaces except a small, square rudder. It was, however, powered by a large 6-cylinder inline engine driving a propeller of some 8½ ft. (2·59 m.) diameter, suggesting that, despite the primitive appearance of the airframe, it was probably a later design than the Phillips II.

**Roe**   50, 62, 63, 67, 77 & 78
The first of many prizes to be offered by the London *Daily Mail* to advance the cause of aviation in Britain was won in March 1907 by Alliott Verdon Roe (1877–1958) with a large, well-made model biplane based on the successful Wright type. With his £75 prize money, Roe began the construction of a full-size aeroplane of a similar pattern having a 36 ft. 0 in. (10·97 m.) wing span and weighing about 600 lb. (272 kg.) including the

pilot. In the early spring of 1908 this machine made several erratic hops after being towed into the air behind a motor car; by the end of May it had been strengthened, fitted with a 24 h.p. Antoinette engine and given auxiliary winglets between the two mainplanes. Controversy still exists over the nature and extent of this aeroplane's early flights, which took place in June. Roe himself identified 8 June as the date of his first flight, when he flew for about 150 ft. (46 m.). Opinion, recent or contemporary, as to the best flight made in this aircraft varies in its estimates from 60 yd. (55 m.) to about 330 yards (300 m.), but the point is to some extent academic; Roe considered that his first truly successful aircraft was the Type E, which did not appear until nearly four years later. In any event, further development and testing of the 1908 biplane was very soon forestalled when Roe was obliged to vacate his Brooklands workshop.

In new premises beneath the railway arches at Lea Marshes, Hackney, he next began work on a fresh design, of tractor layout with triple wing and tail lifting surfaces. The machine was remarkably compact and light – it had to be, for its engine was only a 6 h.p. J.A.P., even smaller than the one that had failed to get his first machine airborne. Better fortune attended the *Avroplane*, or *Bull's-eye*, as it was variously known,* for after a few short hops

_____
* There was no established *contemporary* nomenclature for the early Roe machines until the appearance of the

in May and June 1909 it began to show improvement. On 23 July 1909 it accomplished a flight of 900 ft. (274 m.), and at Wembley Park in December, now with a 9 h.p. engine, it flew for about half a mile (805 m.). The Mercury, an improved triplane with a 35 h.p. Green engine, 2-blade propeller, 20 ft. 0 in. (6·10 m.) equal-span wings and a plywood-skinned fuselage, was exhibited at the 1910 Aero Show at Olympia by the newly-formed A. V. Roe & Co. Ltd. A second Mercury, completed soon afterward, had the upper and middle mainplanes extended to 31 ft. 0 in. (9·45 m.) span, with lateral control by ailerons instead of wing-warping. Both machines were unfortunately destroyed by fire during a rail journey to the Blackpool meeting in July 1910, but Roe was able, somewhat hastily, to assemble a new machine from spares in time to take part at the meeting. This aircraft, and another triplane built to the order of the Harvard Aeronautical Society, he took to the United States later that year.

Type D biplane in 1911. It seems reasonable to infer that Roe viewed this as basically a modification of the Roe IV triplane; if so, the most logical designation of preceding designs would be Roe I for the 1908 biplane, Roe II for the 1909 triplane and Roe III for the 1910 Mercury and its derivative with extended middle and upper wings. Some sources, however, refer to both the biplane *and* the first triplane as Roe I, the Mercury as the Roe II and its extended-span development as the Roe III.

The Roe IV of 1911 was essentially a further variation on the Mercury theme. It retained the 35 h.p. Green engine and 20 ft. lower wings, but the span of the other two mainplanes was increased slightly and a return made to warp control. A single, fixed tailplane, with hinged elevators, and a 4-wheel, 2-skid undercarriage were fitted. At the end of March it was followed by the Type D, a biplane development of it with a 35 h.p. E.N.V. engine; this began flight trials early in April. A racing version of the Type D with extended-span top wings was entered for the July 1911 Circuit of Britain race, but was damaged when the overhanging sections were wrenched off by strong winds. Another Type D was tested by Naval pilots at Barrow with a twin-float gear and semi-circular rudder. The Type E, or Avro 500, was a much-refined development of the D, the prototype appearing in 1912 with a 60 h.p. E.N.V. engine and a more stream-lined and fully-covered fuselage. One Type E was built with a 50 h.p. Gnome engine for a private customer, and subsequently about eight similarly-powered examples with deepened fuselages were built to War Office contracts. These in turn gave rise to the Avro Type F, a radically different design – a mid-wing cabin monoplane with a fully enclosed rectangular-section fuselage. To compete in the 1912 Military Trials, Roe scaled up the Type F (which was too light and carried too modest a load) into the Type G (sometimes described as the Avro 501) cabin biplane. Plans were made to build two of these aircraft, one with a 60 h.p. Green and the other with an 80 h.p. A.B.C. radial. The former machine was flown in the Trials by Lieutenant Wilfred Parke, and proved to be one of the most reliable aircraft taking part.

The aeroplane which really set the seal on A. V. Roe's pre-war success, and which was later to ensure the expansion and prosperity of his company, was the Avro 504, flown for the first time at Brooklands in July 1913. It was a handsome little 2-bay biplane whose only discordant contour was the lumpy, square-cut cowling of the 80 h.p. Gnome engine, and subsequent modifications brought this to a more pleasing shape. By the time it was flown by F. P. Raynham in the September 1913 Aerial Derby, inversely-tapered warping ailerons had been fitted to both sets of wings, and although the aircraft came only fourth in the contest (with an average speed of 66·5 m.p.h. (107 km/hr.)) it attracted a great deal of favourable comment. Tested at the Royal Aircraft Factory in November 1913, by which time the inversely-tapered original ailerons had been replaced by hinged rectangular ones, it recorded a level speed of 80·9 m.p.h. (130·2 km/hr.), and on 10 February 1914 Raynham set a new British altitude record of 14,420 ft. (4,395 m.). The prototype 504 was eventually destroyed in a take-off crash on 10 August 1914, after it had been bought by the *Daily Mail* and

later re-engined – to its detriment – with a Gnome Monosoupape. By this time, however, its future was virtually assured. In later years, Roe said that when he first designed the 504 he thought he would be lucky to get orders for six; but initial small orders, by both the R.F.C. and the R.N.A.S., were soon followed by more substantial ones, and the Avro 504 remained in production during and after the war until more than ten thousand examples had been built.

**Royal Aircraft Factory** 27, 66, 68 & 69

In April 1911 the former H.M. Balloon Factory was renamed Army Aircraft Factory, and almost exactly a year later the name was changed again, to Royal Aircraft Factory. Up to this time almost all of its early aeroplanes had been wholly or partly designed by Geoffrey de Havilland (*q.v.*). Whether de Havilland had any hand in designing the Factory's radical F.E.3 is problematical but, along with R. C. Kemp and S. C. Wingfield Smith, he was certainly one of the test pilots who flew it during 1913. Design of the F.E.3 had begun at the end of the previous year as an attempt at a 2-seat fighter and night bomber with a gun armament. The current belief favoured a pusher layout, so that the observer/gunner could occupy the front cockpit with a range of vision and fire unrestricted by the engine or its whirling propeller. In the F.E.3 a 1½ pdr. Coventry Ordnance Works gun was installed in the front of the pod-shaped fuselage, to fire through an opening in the nose. The 100 h.p. Chenu engine was also mounted well forward, with a shaft drive along the fuselage floor to a vertical chain reduction gear at the rear. This drove the 4-blade pusher propeller, which rotated on a tubular shaft that passed through its centre and served as the tail support boom. During flight trials the F.E.3 showed quite a good performance, but the tailboom's lack of rigidity was considered a dangerous feature, and the aircraft's activities were soon confined to ground firing tests of the C.O.W. gun. Early in 1914 the Factory produced the F.E.6, a refined and enlarged version with a 120 h.p. Austro-Daimler engine, wing span of 49 ft. 4¾ in. (15·05 m.) and gross weight of 2,630 lb. (1,193 kg.). However, by this time it had become clear that more orthodox pusher types such as the F.E.2 and the Vickers 'gunbus' were preferred, and further development was abandoned.

While only in his middle twenties, Henry Folland was the leader of a design department at the Royal Aircraft Factory, charged with continuing development of the B.S.1/ S.E.2 tractor biplane (see the de Havilland entry on page 119). Folland was a meticulous designer, and the care that he took over the smallest detail was evident in the excellent finish of the S.E.4 single-seat biplane that appeared in 1914. The performance already exhibited by the S.E.2a had convinced Folland that a developed version could become the fastest aeroplane yet to be flown. The S.E.4, as the new

machine was designated (S.E.3 having been a projected but un-built development of the S.E.2a), incorporated many advanced features. Among these were a circular-section fuselage (though built-up around a typical box-girder frame), a transparent celluloid cockpit canopy, and variable-camber wings whose rear surfaces, along almost the whole span, could be flexed in flight or lowered to act as landing flaps. Special drag-reducing features included single I-pattern interplane struts, streamlined bracing wires, an NACA cowling for the engine, a large conical spinner for the 4-blade propeller, and fairings on the wheels and axle. Even the gaps between the ailerons, elevators and rudder and their adjacent fixed surfaces were bridged by an elastic mesh. Powerplant was a two-row Gnome rotary developing 160 h.p.

The S.E.4 was as advanced for 1914 as the B.S.1 had been in 1912. When flown in June by Norman Spratt, one of the Factory's test pilots, it showed first-class flying characteristics, although no pilot who flew it could be persuaded to use the transparent hood. Folland had however achieved his ambition to produce a faster aeroplane than anyone else: the S.E.4. showed the astounding figures of more than 1,600 ft/min. (8·13 m/sec) in the climb and 135 m.p.h. (217 km/hr.) in level flight. The latter figure was an unofficial world record, although never claimed as such, and had been matched by very few other aircraft in existence when the war ended four years later. The chief problem was overheating of the big, powerful engine, whose cooling system was seriously hampered by the large spinner originally fitted. To overcome this an aperture was cut in the tip of the spinner, inside which a small cooling fan was installed; but this did not resolve the problem entirely. The S.E.4 was given the official serial number 628 and taken over by the R.F.C., but its further development was abandoned after a section of the undercarriage was damaged during a landing, and it saw no operational service.

In 1916 the Royal Aircraft Factory produced four examples of another single-seat biplane with the designation S.E.4a. These also had full-span aileron/flap surfaces, but otherwise bore a closer resemblance to Folland's later S.E.5 than to the S.E.4. Powerplant was a fully-cowled 80 h.p. Gnome, and the 2-blade propeller had a shallow, bowl-shaped spinner similar to that fitted to the Bristol M.1C. The wings were braced with pairs of parallel interplane struts, and the S.E.4a carried an armament of one rifle.

## Santos-Dumont 4 & 36

Alberto Santos-Dumont, the Brazilian expatriate who played a leading part in making Europe air-minded at the beginning of the century, came to Paris in 1898. During that year he built his No. 1, a non-rigid airship some 82 ft. (25 m.) long and driven by a 3½ h.p. petrol engine. This engine, and other components from No. 1, went into the slightly larger No. 2, also

completed in 1898. In fact, twelve of Santos-Dumont's first twenty designs – not all of which flew or were even built – were airships, all except the first two being of the semi-rigid variety. (There was, incidentally, no design No. 8, Santos having a superstitious fear of this figure which also made him refuse to fly on the 8th of any month.)

The event which first brought Santos-Dumont into the public limelight took place in October 1901, when he flew his 108 ft. (33 m.), 20 h.p. airship No. 6 from St. Cloud, round the Eiffel Tower and back to his starting point in half an hour to win the 150,000 frs. Deutsch Prize. In 1905 he built a monoplane glider, the No. 11, which underwent brief tests towed behind a motor launch; its design was subsequently revised with the object of turning it into a powered aeroplane, but no engine was ever fitted to it. Santos also completed a mock-up of a twin-rotor helicopter, the No. 12, but through lack of a suitable powerplant this was never tested.

There followed two further airships, the Nos. 13 and 14, before, inspired by the Wright brothers' achievements, Santos-Dumont evolved his first powered aeroplane. This was the 14bis, so called because it was briefly tested in 1906 suspended beneath the No. 14 airship. Prior to this it had been given an even more primitive 'trial', being suspended from an overhead wire and towed along by a donkey. Built at Neuilly-Saint-James, the 14bis followed a canard layout, exhibiting a mixture of Wright and Hargrave influence in its forward elevators and boxkite wings. The latter were rigged with some 10 degrees of dihedral, the lower (and therefore longer) mainplanes each measuring 5·75 m. from root to tip. From this the wing span of the 14bis is often given as 11·50 m., but after allowing for the reduction due to dihedral the actual horizontal distance between wingtips was nearer 11·20 m. A small box cellule at the front of the machine, pivoted on a universal joint, performed as a rudder when moved to left or right and as an elevator when moved up or down. In its original form the 14bis was fitted with a 24 h.p. Antoinette engine driving a pusher propeller, and on 13 September 1906, at Bagatelle, it made its first free, powered take-off. After travelling about 23 ft. (7 m.), however, it landed again heavily and was damaged. The framework was repaired, a 50 h.p. Antoinette fitted, and on 23 October the 14bis again took to the air. On this occasion it made a flight of 197 ft. (60 m.) in 7 seconds, qualifying for the 3,000 frs. prize offered by Archdeacon in 1904 for the first aircraft in Europe to cover a distance of 25 m. Less than three weeks later Santos-Dumont had collected another 1,500 frs., this time offered by the Aéro Club de France for the first aeroplane to fly more than 100 m. The 14bis now incorporated a small octagonal aileron in each outer wing cell to improve lateral control. Santos made altogether six flights with the aileron-fitted 14bis at Bagatelle on 12 November 1906, and the longest

of these qualified for the Aéro Club's prize. Lasting 21·2 seconds, it carried 722 ft. (220 m.) at a height of some 20 ft. (6 m.). The control wires actuating the ailerons emanated from a body harness worn by the pilot, so that if one wing of the aircraft dipped, he had only to lean in the opposite direction to bring the machine back on to an even keel.

In context, the flights of the 14bis were modest in the extreme, and the aeroplane itself far from practical in terms of control or performance, yet historically they rank as the first officially recognised aeroplane flights in Europe. Their true value lies not in their intrinsic performance, but in the effect they had in convincing the European public at large that the aeroplane had at last 'arrived'. Indicative of this wider enthusiasm was the handsome prize of 12,500 frs. (about £500), offered early in December 1906 by one of France's most respected vintners to the first airman to make a cross-Channel flight. Two and a half years later, when Louis Blériot accomplished such a flight, he wrote to Santos 'I only followed and imitated you. For us aviators your name is a banner. You are our pathfinder'.

Santos-Dumont was evidently well aware of the limitations of the 14bis, for his next design in sequence, the No. 15, adopted a tractor layout. Unfortunately, it crashed during its first attempt to take off, and neither it nor a proposed development, the No. 17, were taken further. Two other intermediate designs of 1907 were another airship, the No. 16, and a wingless hydroplane, the No.

18, which underwent taxying tests on the Seine. But the aircraft which reflect most credit on Santos-Dumont as a designer are the little single-seaters known collectively by the name *Demoiselle* (Dragonfly). What we may regard as the prototype for the *Demoiselle* was the No. 19, flown at Bagatelle in November 1907. Powered by an 18–20 h.p. Dutheil-Chalmers engine mounted over the centre-section of its dihedral wings, the No. 19 can justifiably be regarded as the world's first really successful light aircraft, weighing only some 107 kg. (235 lb.) without its pilot. Its 'fuselage' consisted of a single bamboo boom, bearing at the rear a cruciform tail unit on a universal pivot that enabled it to function both as an elevator and as a rudder. Beneath the wings was mounted the 3-wheeled chassis and the pilot's seat, abreast of which were two auxiliary rudders outboard of the canted main pair of landing wheels. On its first flight, the No. 19 covered 623 ft. (190 m.), improving this to 656 ft. (200 m.) on its second flight, made at Issy-les-Moulineaux on 17 November 1907. The aircraft made only one more flight, at Buc four days later, but after covering some 492 ft. (150 m.) the propeller was broken when it made a crash-landing. Santos replaced it, but so far as is known it made no further flights.

In November 1908, Santos completed a modified machine known as the 19*bis*, which differed principally by having a 24 h.p. Antoinette Vee-type engine, mounted between the wheels of the chassis with a belt drive to the silk-covered 2-blade propeller, and by dispensing with the auxiliary rudders. No evidence has been found that the 19*bis* ever flew, but in any event completion of the far superior No. 20 *Demoiselle* was imminent. In the No. 20, Santos reverted to a Dutheil-Chalmers engine, which he had had built by Darracq to his own modifications to give 35 h.p. This was restored to its original location above the centre-section and drove a 2-blade Chauvière mahogany propeller. A novel feature was the radiator, which consisted of a series of parallel tubes running beneath the lower wing close to the fuselage. Water entered these tubes at the top edge and ran down to a receiver at the back, where it was then pumped back again to the engine. The rear framework of the *Demoiselle* was made sturdier by three bamboo struts, forming a triangular section to support the tail assembly, and the wings – rather greater in area than those of the No. 19 – were warp-controlled by a vertical rod connected to a body harness. The controls were sensitive, and it was not an easy machine to handle except in the calmest weather conditions, but it achieved some noteworthy performances. The first flight was made at Issy on 6 March 1909; a month later $1\frac{1}{4}$ miles (2 km.) was recorded; and in September Santos made a 16 minute flight in which he covered 11 miles (18 km.). The No. 20 (not the 19*bis* as is sometimes claimed) was exhibited on the Clément-Bayard stand in the

*Grand Palais* in Paris later that month.

During 1909 and 1910 the *Demoiselle* found a modest market among fliers seeking a small 'sporting' machine. Between ten and fifteen were probably built, some of which will have been of the No. 21 or No. 22 type. The unfortunate destruction by Santos of his personal records in 1914 leaves a little confusion over the exact differences between these variants. The No. 21 has been described as having a Darracq engine, though more probably this was still the Darracq-built modification of the Dutheil-Chalmers. The No. 22 was larger and more robust, powered by a 40 h.p. Clément-Bayard engine, for which a maximum speed of about 68 m.p.h. (110 km/hr.) was claimed.

Sadly, the *Demoiselle* was Santos-Dumont's first and last really successful aeroplane. His last known flight as a pilot was made in November 1909, and in spring 1910 his retirement was precipitated by the onset of the multiple sclerosis that was to beset him for the rest of his life. Shortly before this he achieved the unique distinction of being the only aviator to hold a licence to fly four different types of aircraft – monoplanes, biplanes, airships and balloons – but for the next two decades, until his tragic suicide in 1932, his life was clouded by ill-health and much self-inflicted mental agony. None of this, however, could detract from what Santos-Dumont achieved in the first ten years of the century, ably summarised by his English biographer,

Peter Wykeham: 'He opened the door in Europe, and the crowds streamed through.'

**Short**   20, 21, 60 & 73

The three Short brothers – Horace, Eustace and Oswald – united in 1908 to form the first company in Britain for the commercial production of aeroplanes. Their association with the air began nearly a decade before this, Eustace Short being an ardent balloonist and enlisting his younger brother's aid in manufacturing them during the early years of the century. It was Wilbur Wright's tour of France in 1908 that persuaded them to turn to heavier-than-air machines, and at the beginning of 1909 the brothers' reputation for excellent workmanship earned them a licence to build six Wright Flyers for British customers. Prior to this, however, Horace Short had already begun the design of a pusher-type biplane at the company's 'offices' under the railway arches at Battersea. It was exhibited, though in an unfinished state, at Olympia in March 1909, and was eventually completed during the summer. Like the Wright design on which it was broadly based, it required a launching rail in order to take off, but it incorporated several variations from the standard Wright machine. The Short No. 1 weighed about 1,200 lb. (544 kg.) and had a wing span of 40 ft. 0 in. (12·19 m.). It was completed at new premises near Leysdown, on the Isle of Sheppey, and attempts were made to fly it, first with a 30 h.p. Nordenfeld motor car engine and then with a Bariquand & Marre engine of similar output, but the aircraft barely reached the end of its launching rail and never got into the air. (The belief that it later flew successfully with a Green engine is nowadays discounted.)

The Short brothers' next two designs were somewhat closer to the general Wright pattern, with the important distinction that they featured between-wing ailerons instead of the Wrights' wing-warping system. The Short No. 2 was built for J. T. C. Moore-Brabazon and was first flown on 27 September 1909 with a 30 h.p. Vivinus engine; it, too, was launched from a rail. Shortly afterwards a 60 h.p. Green was substituted, and, thus powered, it was flown by Moore-Brabazon on the first 1-mile circuit flight made in the United Kingdom, on 30 October. (A much-published photograph of Moore-Brabazon shows him with the piglet that he once took up as a passenger to refute the 'pigs might fly' epithet so beloved by opponents of flying; the flight concerned took place on 4 November 1909 and was made in the Short No. 2.) The No. 2 was on show at Olympia in March 1910, with a single directly-coupled propeller in place of the original chain-driven pair, and after the Show Moore-Brabazon used it in a successful bid to win the British Empire Michelin Cup. The Short No. 3 was also at Olympia. This had been built for the Hon. C. S. Rolls, and theoretically should have been a better aeroplane than the No. 2. Smaller and lighter than Brabazon's machine, it had a retrac-

ting 4-wheel landing gear and was powered by a 35 h.p. Green engine; but it would not fly, and the five similar aircraft ordered before the Olympia Show were never started.

April 1910 saw the Shorts transfer their activities to Eastchurch, and the design and manufacture of aeroplanes began in earnest. The first Eastchurch type was the S.27, and in it the Shorts deserted the Wright layout for the increasingly popular and successful formula established by Henry Farman the year before. Several machines of the S.27 type were built, all to the basic Farman pattern, but differing in powerplant and various design features according to customer requirements. Among the earliest customers was F. K. McClean, for whom the original No. 1 had been built and whose encouragement and support were to a very large extent responsible for the successful establishment of the Shorts' business. A modified S. 27, fitted with pontoons, took off from a platform on the foredeck of H.M.S. *Africa* in Sheerness harbour on 10 January 1912, flown by Lieutenant C. R. Samson, R.N., and on 9 May Samson made another deck take-off, this time from H.M.S. *Hibernia* off Weymouth – the first take-off by a British aircraft from a moving ship. Later that year, on 10 August, McClean flew up the Thames in a float-fitted S.33, passing through the opening of Tower Bridge and beneath every other bridge until he reached Westminster. Later examples of the S.27 type, including the S.35 and S.38, had extended upper wings of 46 ft.

o in. (14·02 m.) span, an enclosed nacelle for the two occupants, and a 50 or 70 h.p. Gnome rotary engine in place of the original E.N.V. The first S.38 was flown on 24 May 1911. Later, in service with the R.F.C. Naval Wing, similar aircraft were concerned in radio-telegraphy experiments and some of the earliest trials with a machine-gun mounted in the front cockpit. A scaled-up development of the S.38, designated S.70, was produced late in 1913. Built to McClean's order for a proposed Egyptian tour, it was a seaplane with two main floats and two smaller tail floats. It had a span of 70 ft. 6 in. (21·49 m.) and was powered by a two-row Gnome pusher of 160 h.p.

Chronologically, however, these types were preceded by a number of unfruitful and somewhat freakish designs, beginning with the Tandem Twin and Triple Twin built in 1911 for Francis McClean. The Tandem Twin was so called because its twin 50 h.p. Gnome engines were mounted in tandem, one at the front and one at the back of the small 2-seat nacelle, driving tractor and pusher propellers respectively. In the Triple Twin the engines were similarly located, but the forward one drove two outboard tractor propellers by means of a chain drive. Both machines were taken over by the Admiralty at the end of the year and used for training. The Tandem Tractor, whose design had been started in 1910 for Cecil Grace and suspended after his death in December, was resurrected in the following autumn and flown in

January 1912. It was a neat, 2-seat, 2-bay biplane with an openwork fuselage, unequal-span wings and a 70 h.p. Gnome engine. In the spring of 1912, with the fuselage covered and a large central float replacing the land undercarriage, it underwent further tests, and was the Shorts' first really successful seaplane. By contrast, the Triple Tractor, with two 50 h.p. Gnomes under a very long nose cowling, was another rather bizarre design. One Gnome drove a directly-coupled propeller, the other a pair of outboard propellers, but when test flights started in July 1912 the engines very soon showed a tendency to overheat.

The Shorts' next significant product was the 2/3-seat S.41, a twin-float biplane, which, like the Tandem Tractor, had a conventional fuselage instead of the Farman-type arrangement of tailbooms. It was originally completed with a land undercarriage, but this was soon replaced by the float gear. Three were built for the R.F.C. Naval Wing with 100 h.p. Gnome engines. Improved S.41 types followed, these being typified by Admiralty No. 42 (2-bay wings and 80 h.p. Gnome) and Type 74 (3-bay wings and 100 h.p. Gnome). The specialised development of marine aircraft was now established as the Shorts' true *métier*, and another notable advance in this field came in 1913 when Horace Short designed a mechanism to make a seaplane's wings fold back alongside the fuselage, so that it could be stored easily on board a warship. The Short Folder, as the new type was simply titled, entered R.N.A.S. service in mid-1913, and in one Folder, on 28 July 1914, Squadron Commander A. M. Longmore carried out an air launching of a torpedo for the first time in Britain. Larger wing-folding Short seaplanes followed, including Admiralty Types 135 (135 h.p. Salmson), 136 and 166 (200 h.p. Salmson). Six of the last-named type were completed for the R.N.A.S. in 1914, and a batch were also built by Westland.

The Shorts had not quite finished with pusher types, for in 1913 they had produced a 2-seat 'gunbus', the S.81, with a 160 h.p. Gnome and a Vickers 1½ pdr. gun; in 1915 it was used also in tests of the 6 pdr. Davis gun.

## Sikorsky 72

Igor Ivanovich Sikorsky, renowned for more than a quarter of a century as one of the world's foremost helicopter designers, was born in Kiev in 1889. His first attempts at helicopter construction, in 1909–10, were unsuccessful, and he then turned his attention to fixed-wing aircraft, designing a series of small, moderately successful biplanes for the Imperial Russian Army air service. Late in 1912, with the collaboration of G. I. Lavrov, he embarked on a considerably more ambitious project – the world's first 4-engined aeroplane. Dubbed *Le Grand*\* (The Great One) by the

---

\* The word *Bolsche* is often applied in relation to this aircraft: the meaning is the same, although the correct nominative form (*Bolsche* being the adjectival form) should be *Bolschoi*.

factory staff, it was built in six months and made its maiden flight at St. Petersburg, with Sikorsky and Aleknovich as pilots, on 13 May 1913. Apart from sheer size *Le Grand* had many advanced features, including dual controls and a fully enclosed cabin, generously panelled with unbreakable glass windows, for the passengers and crew. In front of the cabin was an open observation platform, with a searchlight mounted on the extreme nose. A sturdy 4-skid undercarriage was fitted in addition to the 16-wheeled landing gear, and the four 100 h.p. Argus engines were mounted on the lower wings in tandem pairs, each pair driving a 2-blade tractor propeller. The first take-off was somewhat laboured and Sikorsky, dissatisfied with the functioning of the two rear engines, had them moved in June 1913\* to separate locations on the lower leading edges. *Le Grand*, bearing the name *Russkii Knyaz* (Russian Knight), made more than fifty successful flights, including one on 8 August 1913 in which it set up a world endurance record of 1 hr. 54 min. with 8 people on board and reached an altitude of 2,723 ft. (830 m.). In autumn 1913 *Le Grand* was severely damaged when the engine of a Voisin biplane, overflying the Army airfield at Krasnoe Selo, tore loose and crashed on to its wings.

*Le Grand* was then dismantled, for by this time work was about to begin on an even larger aeroplane. Using the same powerplant as *Le*

---

\* The caption on page 89 should read "summer 1913".

*Grand*, the new aircraft had a wing span of 101 ft. 8½ in. (31·00 m.), a wing area of 1,700 sq. ft. (158 sq. m.) and an estimated gross weight of about 10,030 lb. (4,550 kg.). Wings and fuselage were of more efficient design, and a more spacious crew cabin was installed. The long, covered passenger compartment, with a floor area of some 140 sq. ft. (13 sq. m.), was furnished with a sofa, four armchairs and a table at which hot drinks could be served in flight. Other amenities included electric light, cabin heating, a wardrobe and a toilet. Behind the cabin, passengers who were sufficiently intrepid could stroll along the 'promenade deck', actually the top of the fuselage, which was flanked by a handrail on either side. The new aeroplane, named *Ilya Mourometz* after a legendary Russian folk hero, was completed in December 1913 and made its first flight in January 1914. Its landing gear consisted of wide, steel-shod wooden skis; a wheeled undercarriage was not fitted until later. Its carrying capacity was amply demonstrated on 11 February, when it made an 18 minute flight at St. Petersburg carrying 16 passengers – a payload equivalent to some 2,866 lb. (1,300 kg.) – to a height of 985 ft. (300 m.). This was typical of many similar flights made during the early months of the year.

In April 1914 a second, basically similar aeroplane was completed, differing only in having more powerful engines. The inboard pair were each rated at 140 h.p. and the outer pair at 125 h.p. On 18 June 1914 the *Ilya Mourometz* No. 2 established yet another impressive feat of endurance, staying aloft for 6½ hours with 6 passengers on board; and between 29 June and 11 July made an even more remarkable journey, covering the 1,590 miles (2,560 km.) from St. Petersburg to Kiev and back in 10½ hours' flying time with only a single stop for re-fuelling. During this journey, which was not without its hazards, an incidental event was the first occasion on which a complete meal was prepared and served on board an aeroplane.

The Kiev flight brought Sikorsky an order for a batch of *Ilya Mouro-metz* bombers for the Imperial Russian Air Service, to be built by the Russo-Baltic Waggon Factory; while later in July the *Ilya Mourometz* No. 1 made several successful flights at Libava with a Sikorsky-designed twin-float landing gear. No naval orders ensued, but nearly eighty of the landplanes were completed for the I.R.A.S. Their wartime career is described in the *Bombers 1914–19* volume in this series.

**Sopwith** 34 & 70
Thomas Sopwith, founder of the present-day Hawker Siddeley Group, made his first flight as a passenger in a Farman biplane at Brooklands in 1910. He subsequently bought an Avis monoplane, which he crashed, and a Howard-Wright biplane, on which he taught himself to fly. He qualified as a pilot in November 1910, and in the following month won the £4,000 prize offered by Baron de Forest for the

longest flight by an Englishman from England to the Continent (169 miles = 272 km., from Eastchurch to Thirimont in Belgium). In the United States in 1911 he collected more money prizes, and in June 1912, flying a 2-seat Blériot monoplane, won the first United Kingdom Aerial Derby sponsored by the London *Daily Mail*. By this time he was running a flying school at Brooklands, and after the disappointment of the Coventry Ordnance Works biplane which he flew in the Military Trials in August, Sopwith began to think in terms of building aircraft of his own.

His first venture was to modify one of the Brooklands machines, a Burgess-Wright biplane, by fitting it with a 40 h.p. A.B.C. radial engine. It was flown by the Australian Harry Hawker, whom Sopwith taught to fly and who soon became the company's chief pilot. Hawker progressed from pupil to record breaker in seven weeks, for in October he won the £500 British Empire Michelin Trophy for 1912 with a flight lasting 8 hr. 23 min. – a new British endurance record that was still unsurpassed by the beginning of World War 1 nearly two years later. Sopwith's second machine was a hybrid affair, a tractor biplane based again on the wing arrangement of the Burgess-Wright, but fitted with a Farman-type undercarriage and using the 70 h.p. Gnome engine from the school's Blériot monoplane. It crashed during an early flight, but was rebuilt with a fully-covered fuselage, simplified undercarriage and other refinements and sold to the Admiralty in October 1912.

The first truly original design to emerge from the new company was also one of considerable significance to British aviation, for it was the first hull-type British flying boat and, as modified later, one of the first amphibious flying boats designed in Europe. Following the example of Curtiss, Sopwith had a beautifully streamlined 21 ft. (6·40 m.) hull designed and built by S. E. Saunders. Equal-span biplane wings were mounted on top of this with a 90 h.p. Austro-Daimler engine driving a pusher propeller, and the twin-rudder tail unit supported by outrigged booms. Before its appearance at the Olympia Aero Show in February 1913, the Bat Boat, as the aircraft had been named, had been modified by lengthening the tail-booms and fitting a twin-wheel land undercarriage that could be raised above water level. It was test-flown at Cowes shortly afterwards, and Sopwith then set his sights on the £500 Mortimer Singer prize for amphibians. To qualify for this an English powerplant was necessary, and so the Austro-Daimler was replaced by a 100 h.p. Green; the forward elevator was also removed. In this form, it competed successfully on 9 July 1913. After the competition the original engine was restored, the undercarriage removed and the aircraft sold to the Admiralty. It crashed in August 1913, but an immediate replacement was ordered. An enlarged version, the Bat Boat 2, appeared at Olympia in March 1914. This was a 'pure' flying boat, with a mahogany-skinned hull, 200 h.p. Salmson radial engine and gross weight of 3,180 lb. (1,442 kg.). The lower wings had pronounced dihedral, and the span of the upper ones was increased to 55 ft. 0 in. (16·76 m.). Howard Pixton was to have flown the Bat Boat 2 in the 1914 Circuit of Britain race, but the event was forestalled by the onset of war in Europe.

Another excellent Sopwith exhibit at the 1913 Aero Show had been a 3-seat tractor biplane, described in contemporary reports as 'beautifully engineered and constructed'. Powered only by an 80 h.p. Gnome engine, it was flown by Hawker in some remarkable high altitude performances, and was the subject of production contracts for both the Military and Naval Wings of the R.F.C. On 31 May 1913, Hawker set a new British solo altitude record in this aircraft of 11,450 ft. (3,490 m.); on 16 June he flew to 12,900 ft. (3,932 m.) carrying one passenger; and on 27 July to 8,400 ft. (2,560 m.) with three passengers. A batch of similar aircraft were built as 2-seaters for the R.F.C. The Sopwith Type C, a twin-float seaplane with a 200 h.p. Salmson engine, was developed for Admiralty trials with a torpedo launching gear devised by Captain Murray Sueter; this was flown late in 1913.

The Sopwith 3-seater was the ancestor of an even more remarkable aircraft – the 2-seat Tabloid. Known officially as the Type S.S., this was conceived as a faster, scaled-down demonstration version of the 3-

seater for Hawker to take with him to Australia at the end of 1913. Completed at the new Kingston works, it was erected at Brooklands, where it made a successful first flight towards the end of November. A few days later, on 29 November, it was put through measured trials at the Royal Aircraft Factory, Farnborough, where it clocked 92 m.p.h. (148 km/hr.) in level flight and 1,200 ft/min. (6·10 m/sec.) in the climb – better than de Havilland's B.S. 1 and with only an 80 h.p. Gnome for power. Single-seat Tabloids were later built in substantial numbers for the R.F.C. and R.N.A.S. (see the *Fighters 1914–19* volume). The first few production machines, like the original, had wing-warping and balanced rudders, but ailerons soon became standard and a non-balanced rudder was employed in conjunction with a small, fixed triangular fin. At Hendon in February 1914, Howard Pixton flew a specially enlarged 100 h.p. version called the Sociable, built for Winston Churchill. In April, in a special twin-float Tabloid with a 100 h.p. Gnome Monosoupape engine, Pixton swept the board at the 1914 Schneider Trophy meeting with a course average of nearly 87 m.p.h. (140 km/hr.), going on to fly two extra laps and set a new world's speed record for seaplanes of 92 m.p.h. (148 km/hr.). A landplane version of this machine later flew at a speed of 105 m.p.h. (169 km/hr.).

## Vickers 49

The Aviation Department of Vickers, under the management of

Captain H. F. Wood, made its first essays into aeroplane production with a modified version of an R.E.P. monoplane, whose manufacturing rights it acquired early in 1911. Eight of these were completed, the various modifications between them being concerned chiefly with the forward fuselage and landing gear. The first five were fitted with R.E.P. engines and had Farman-style undercarriages. Vickers No. 1, built to the order of the Australian Antarctic Expedition, was flown by Wood in July 1911, but wrecked very soon afterwards by another pilot. To avoid adverse publicity, No. 2 was quickly substituted and left for Australia almost immediately. The third, fourth and fifth machines followed the same broad pattern. Vickers No. 6, nicknamed the 'Sociable', was a more radical departure from the R.E.P. pattern, having side-by-side seats with dual controls, a twin-wheel and single-skid undercarriage and a 70 h.p. Viale radial engine. This unit, after giving trouble during the 1912 Military Trials, was succeeded by a 70 h.p. Gnome. A modified version of the Gnome-engined model appeared at the February 1913 Aero Show as Vickers No. 8 (No. 7 having been a 100 h.p. Gnome development of No. 5).

Design of the No. 6 monoplane had been largely the work of A. R. Low and G. H. Challenger, who also produced in 1912 the Hydravion, or Vickers No. 14. This twin-float pusher biplane, with its 100 h.p. Gnome engine and 73 ft. 0 in. (22·25 m.) wing span, was at the

time the largest aircraft in Britain but crashed on an early test flight and was not rebuilt. Another short-lived venture was a 70 h.p. Gnome-powered 2-seat tractor biplane, which crashed into the Thames in January 1913 only a month after being completed.

The Vickers company is probably best known during this period for its evolution of a successful 'gunbus' military biplane. It stemmed from an Admiralty requirement issued in November 1912 and, like other contemporary efforts to develop a gun-carrying aeroplane, assumed a pusher engine configuration so as to place the observer in the front with an uninterrupted field of vision and fire. Exhibited at Olympia in February 1913 as the Type 18 'Destroyer', it attracted much attention for its heavily-staggered wings (which, even at this late date, were warp-controlled) and well-rounded 2-seat nacelle. An 80 h.p. Wolseley engine was installed at the rear of this nacelle, while in the front cockpit a Vickers-Maxim machine gun was mounted to fire through a slot in the nose that permitted it to be traversed through some 60 degrees from left to right or elevated and depressed to a similar extent. An accident to this prototype, later designated E.F.B.1 (Experimental Fighting Biplane No. 1), led Low to simplify the design in the E.F.B.2 by eliminating the wing stagger, fitting a less complex undercarriage and installing a 100 h.p. Gnome Mono-soupape engine in a shorter nacelle. This performed satisfactorily in autumn 1913, reaching about 65 m.p.h. (105 km/hr.) during tests. The design was refined still further, the E.F.B.3 (shown at Olympia in March 1914) exhibiting equal-span wings with a full set of ailerons and the E.F.B.5 having the gun firing over the cockpit coaming from a more convenient pillar mounting that gave the observer/gunner a freer range of movement. (The E.F.B.4 was a somewhat bizarre project that was never built.) With other structural modifications the 'Gunbus' then went into production as the F.B.5, described in the *Fighters 1914–19* volume. Vickers' other exhibit at Olympia in 1914, a 2-seat tractor scout designed to emulate the Sopwith Tabloid, was not in the same class as the Tabloid or the Bristol Scout, and was abandoned in favour of 'Gunbus' production and other design projects such as the developed Barnwell E.S.1 'Bullet'.

## Voisin 9, 10 & 11

By their establishment at Billancourt early in 1906 for the manufacture of powered aeroplanes, the Voisin brothers Gabriel (born 1880) and Charles (1882–1912) have the distinction of being the first commercial constructors of aircraft in Europe. They preferred, however, to build reliable but unspectacular machines rather than to risk the uncertainty of experiment. Despite assertions to the contrary by Gabriel in his acrimonious (and often inaccurate) autobiography, the improvements that did appear in Voisin aircraft between 1908 and 1910 almost certainly owed far

more to Henry Farman (*q.v.*) than to the Voisins.

Nevertheless, by their very existence the Voisin biplanes played an important part in the growth of the flying movement in Europe, and many leading aviators had their first taste of flying in a Voisin machine. They are also significant historically as the first practical aircraft to introduce the boxkite configuration of the Australian Lawrence Hargrave. The first association of Gabriel Voisin (the dominant partner) with flying machines dates from early 1904, when he built the first of two biplane gliders, which was flown by the French sportsman Ernest Archdeacon. The second was tested in March 1905 and was followed three months later by two floatplane gliders, which were the first to incorporate the boxkite principle. The first of these flew no more than 985 ft. (300 m.) and a broadly similar machine built for Louis Blériot crashed on its first take-off in July. Another unpowered aircraft, tested in May 1907, was a Chanute-type 'hang-glider' – i.e., the pilot hung beneath it and controlled its movement by swinging his body from side to side.

The Voisins' first powered aeroplane, completed in March 1907, was built for Henry Kapferer, but never flew. It had a 20 h.p. Buchet engine and, like the Archdeacon and Blériot gliders, was based broadly on the Wright concept with equal-span wings and a frontal elevator. Unlike the Wright biplanes, however, the Voisin machine had no built-in lateral control. The basic pattern for the early Voisins was introduced with a machine built at about the same time for Léon Delagrange. This had a wide-span tail 'box' with twin rudders, a biplane front elevator, and with a 50 h.p. Antoinette pusher engine was more effectively powered. Its 32 ft. 9¾ in. (10·00 m.) wings were of equal span, but had no side-curtains and no other form of lateral control. Its best early hop was 197 ft. (60 m.) at Bagatelle in spring 1907; there then followed an unsuccessful attempt to take off, with floats, from the Lac d'Enghien, after which the wheel undercarriage was restored and further flights were made. At Issy on 3 November 1907 it flew for 1,640 ft. (500 m.), but then crashed and was severely damaged. A second biplane was built for Delagrange, possibly from the wreckage of the first, and incorporated modifications similar to those made by Henry Farman to his first Voisin – a single-surface front elevator, slight wing dihedral, and a tail of greatly reduced span. During the first half of 1908 this machine was flown extensively in France and Italy, its best flight being some 8¾ miles (14 km.) at Milan on 23 June. The addition of side-curtains and the increase of interplane gap, made during 1908, brought no appreciable improvement.

Farman, meanwhile, had been making history with the Voisin which he had ordered in June 1907. Slightly bigger and heavier than Delagrange's machine, with a single-cell tail 'box' and only one rudder, it was later modified in various ways by Farman.

The boxkite wing and tail formula, while unspectacular in terms of performance, had yielded a safe and stable aeroplane, although the degree of lateral control which could be exercised was still minimal. But Voisin Frères were happy enough with the orders that were coming in; seven Voisins were entered in the events at Rheims in August 1909, and by the end of the year nearly a score of these aircraft had been built for various customers. One of the earliest was J. T. C. Moore-Brabazon's *Bird of Passage*, first flown on 7 March 1909. This had actually been commissioned by Henry Farman, and it was Voisin's action of selling it instead to Moore-Brabazon (who did not know of Farman's order) that stirred Farman to branch out on his own. The Voisin biplanes flew with a wide variety of engines that included 50 h.p. versions of the Antoinette, E.N.V., Gnome, Itala, Renault and Vivinus, and 60 h.p. versions of the E.N.V., Gobron and Wolseley. Louis Paulhan's Voisin, which took part in the Easter 1909 meeting at Monaco, was the first aeroplane to fly with the new Gnome rotary engine.

The boxkite Voisins remained the standard product during 1910, though the front elevator disappeared and aileron controls were introduced on developed versions. Then, in 1911, there appeared a curious canard design recalling that flown by Santos-Dumont (*q.v.*) five years earlier. Originally this aircraft had a wheeled undercarriage, but during the summer it was mounted on two pairs of Fabre floats. At the beginning of August it was flown from Issy by Colliex, who landed on the Seine at Billancourt, took off again and returned to Issy. In its original form the Voisin canard had an openwork fuselage, square front rudder, equal-span wings with double ailerons and a single outboard pair of side-curtains; its powerplant was a 70 h.p. Gnome. In 1912 a developed version with covered fuselage and possibly a 100 h.p. Gnome was the first aircraft to be ordered by the *Marine Nationale*.

The Voisin company subsequently built almost exclusively to military contracts, producing the sturdy, metal-framed nacelle-and-tailboom pusher biplanes that formed the nucleus of France's bomber and reconnaissance force before and during the early part of World War 1. These are described in the *Bombers 1914–19* volume, and during their early career were concerned in some of the first tests involving the mounting of a machine-gun in the front cockpit. One was also tested with a 37 mm. Hotchkiss cannon, but the first hint of a Voisin 'gunbus' came at the Paris *Salon* of October 1910 when one of the earlier-type biplanes was displayed with a quick-firing gun mounted in front of the pilot.

## Vuia 38

Trajan Vuia was a Paris-domiciled lawyer and engineer from the former Austro-Hungarian province of Tran-

sylvania (now a part of Rumania). The aircraft that he built and flew in 1906–7 were, in themselves, failures, but have been credited with establishing 'the beginning of the European monoplane configuration' and influencing Louis Blériot, among others, in the successful pursuit of the tractor monoplane formula.

Vuia's No. I aeroplane was characterised chiefly by its bat-like wings, which were warp-controlled and (in lieu of a rear elevator) able to have their angle of incidence altered in flight by the pilot. Beneath the wings the chassis consisted of a steel-tube pyramid structure supporting the engine, pilot, rear rudder and four-wheeled landing gear. This last feature was, incidentally, the first aeroplane undercarriage to be fitted with pneumatic tyres; the two front wheels, which were steerable, also controlled the rudder movement. The engine was a Serpollet carbonic acid gas unit, developing 25 h.p. and driving a 2-blade fabric-covered propeller made by Victor Tatin. Wing area of the Vuia I was 215·3 sq. ft. (20 sq. m.), and the aircraft weighed 531 lb. (241 kg.) loaded. Its first flight was made at Montesson on 3 March 1906; four other flights were made, there and at Issy, in July, August and October. The best of these was also the last, since the aircraft crash-landed after covering a distance of 78¾ ft. (24 m.).

In rebuilding it as the No. I*bis*, Vuia discarded the variable-incidence wing control in favour of a more conventional rear elevator in the shape of an elongated triangle. He also reduced the wing camber, but increased the chord, so that, with the same span, it now had an area of 247·6 sq. ft. (23 sq. m.); the elevator was 32·3 sq. ft. (3 sq. m.) in area. The Vuia I*bis* was first flown at Issy on 6 October 1906, and eight days later made its best hop, of 32·8 ft. (10 m.). Up to 30 March 1907, the I*bis* made altogether eight take-offs, some at Issy and the others at Bagatelle.

Vuia's final venture was the No. II, a modified form of the I*bis* in which he substituted a 24 h.p. 8-cylinder Antoinette piston-engine. This, too, was a failure, making only two short hops at Bagatelle in June and July 1907. The second and best of these was no more than 65·6 ft. (20 m.), and in the face of these discouraging results Vuia lacked the enthusiasm (and the technical know-how) to continue his experiments. They had done enough, however, to focus European aviators' attention again on the tractor type of mono-plane, and indirectly led to the emergence of later, successful air-craft designed to such a layout.

**Wright**   5, 6, 7 & 26
Today it is so readily taken for granted that 'everybody knows' that the first genuine powered flights were made by the Wright brothers in 1903 that one tends to forget that not until 1942 was the pre-eminence of their achievement recognised officially by that respected American body, the Smithsonian Institution. It may also be as well to reaffirm exactly what, at this point, they had

achieved, which was the making of the first *controlled and sustained* flight by a powered aeroplane; not for another two years could they (or did they) claim to have developed a fully *practical* aeroplane. But by then they were so far ahead of the fumbling European pioneers that the latter could accept only with a poor grace the reports of the Wrights' progress – until Wilbur Wright came to France in 1908 and showed them.

Both Orville (1871–1948) and Wilbur Wright (1867–1912) are rightly acknowledged for their pains-taking and methodical scientific approach to the problems of flight. Although powered flight was always their ultimate goal, they prepared the ground thoroughly, first by reading every available piece of literature on the subject and then by working matters out for themselves by building gliders on which they taught themselves the craft of pilotage. They made their machines deliberately unstable, so that volun-tary control by the pilot was essential, and this was the corner-stone of their success. The method of control was the simple but effective one of warping, or twisting, the outer ends of the wings in opposing directions, a principle first tried out in a kite that they built in 1899. In October 1900 their first glider was flown (usually without a pilot) at Kitty Hawk, and in July/August 1901 at the nearby Kill Devil Hills the larger Wright No. 2 glider was flown with one or other of the brothers lying prone across the lower wing. There then followed a period of reappraisal during which they rejected the theories and calculations of Otto Lilienthal (on which their own had hitherto been founded) and indulged in a fresh programme of research and aerodynamic testing based on their own experiments, which reached fruition in the No. 3 glider flown in September/October 1902. Once the original pair of fixed rear fins on this machine were replaced by a single controllable rudder this performed to the Wrights' highest expectations and they were ready to consider a powered machine.

This set them a fresh problem, for no existing internal combustion engine that could offer sufficient power was light enough for the task. The Wrights therefore had to design, not only the aeroplane but the engine and the propellers as well. The propellers, in particular, were remarkably efficient considering the almost complete lack of knowledge of this subject; in Europe, propellers of comparable efficiency did not begin to appear for at least another five years. Work on the Wright Flyer I was started in the summer of 1903, and it followed generally the pattern of the No. 3 glider except that it had twin rear rudders and a biplane elevator at the front. After an unsuccessful attempt at flight by Wilbur Wright on 14 December the Flyer I made its first proper take-off three days later with Orville at the controls. Altogether it flew four times that day, the longest flight being of 59 seconds, made by Wilbur and covering more than half a mile (0·80 km.) through the air. It was

nearly four years before Henry Farman, in the Voisin-Farman I, made a better flight than this in Europe, lasting $1\frac{1}{4}$ min. – and by that time the Wright aeroplane could stay aloft for about three-quarters of an hour.

The second biplane, or Flyer II, was flown for the first time on 23 May 1904. The Wrights' flying was now done from the Huffman Prairie, a site with more privacy but less unrestricted space than the Kill Devil Hills, and where take-offs were dependent upon suitable weather conditions. Early in September 1904, therefore, the Wrights introduced a form of assisted take-off to overcome this restriction. Their take-off technique hitherto had involved the use of a rail, the aircraft being restrained at one end while the engine was run up and then released to travel along the rail until it became airborne. Originally this system contributed no artificial acceleration during take-off, but at Huffman Prairie a weight-and-derrick apparatus was devised that was used successfully in thousands of subsequent take-offs. Later, on 20 September, the Flyer II made its first circuit flight, and on 9 November 1904 covered $2\frac{3}{4}$ miles (4·50 km.) in a flight lasting over 5 minutes. It was generally similar to the Flyer I, but had a new 16 h.p. Wright engine and reduced wing camber. In 1905, after being offered to, and rejected (unseen) by, both the U.S. and British War Departments, it was broken up.

Various components, including the engine, were utilised in completing the Flyer III. Longitudinal and directional control was much enhanced in this machine by increasing the length of the booms carrying the forward elevator and the rudders, and the Flyer III could bank, turn, circle and perform figure-of-eights with ease. It was the Wrights' first fully practical machine, and had made up to fifty flights by mid-October, two of them lasting over half an hour. Remarkably, there then followed a period of more than $2\frac{1}{2}$ years during which the Wrights did no flying at all. They had achieved a practical aeroplane: they now consolidated the design of this and developed it into the Flyer Type A, capable of taking up a passenger. The next occasion on which either brother went into the air was on 6 May 1908, when Wilbur Wright began to brush up his piloting skill prior to visiting France for a demonstration tour. The significance of this visit, which began in August 1908, can scarcely be overstated. It demonstrated conclusively the superiority of the Americans' work over anything yet accomplished in Europe, which Europe had been reluctant to believe; but, more important still, it showed the European aviators why they had achieved so little, by emphasising the value of voluntary lateral control. How quickly Europe learned the lesson can be gauged by the variety of aeroplanes at the great Rheims meeting only one year later, and by their performances at that meeting.

While Wilbur was busy in Europe – arranging, incidentally, the pro-

duction of Wright biplanes under licence in Britain (by Shorts), France (by Voisin, with Bariquand & Marre engines) and Germany – Orville Wright was demonstrating the Type A Flyer to the U.S. War Department. In America, no less than in Europe, there was no shortage of disbelievers, but in February 1908 the Army had finally awarded the Wrights a contract for an evaluation aircraft. In September it was demonstrated before Signal Corps officials at Fort Myer, Virginia, making ten flights, four of which were over an hour in duration, and proving, as one witness put it, that the Wrights really were fliers, not liars. (Europe's best at that time was 30 minutes 27 seconds by the Voisin-Delagrange III biplane.) The Military Flyer crashed after its tenth flight, on 17 September 1908, but was later rebuilt and returned on 29 June 1909 when fresh military trials were started with it as a faster, shorter-span machine. This was subsequently purchased by the U.S. Army as the Signal Corps No. 1. This machine, along with the original Flyer I, is now in the National Air and Space Museum in Washington.

Later designs included the Type B of 1910, which took off conventionally using a wheel-and-skid undercarriage and was the first Wright type to have no frontal elevator. Two Type B's were supplied to the U.S. Army in 1911. The Type R or Roadster of 1910 was a 30 h.p. civil single-seater, of which the Baby Wright was a smaller racing version. On a modified short-span Roadster,

Ralph Johnstone set up an altitude record of 9,714 ft. (2,998 m.) at Belmont Park, New York, in October 1910. During this meeting the British pilot A. Ogilvie flew a Baby Wright into third place in the race for the Gordon Bennett Trophy. Seven Type C's and two Type D's were built in 1912-13 for the U.S. Army, being respectively 2-seat and single-seat scouts with 50 h.p. Wright engines.

# INDEX

The reference numbers refer to the illustrations and corresponding text.